Going Spiritual:
Discovering, Developing and Healing a Spiritual Life

Rev. John R. Gishler B.A., M.L.S., M.Div.

Dedicated to:
Lucille, who gave me *Something More*;
My children Christopher, David and Mary;
My precious grandchildren Anna, Thomas, Liam, Elliot,
Sophie and Elizabeth;
and all my spiritual children
as signs of the Glory of God.

Contents

Foreword   v

I   Going Spiritual   1

1   Becoming Who You Were Meant to Be   3

2   What is Spiritual Life?   9
- 2.1   Our Bodies 10
- 2.2   The Personal Spirit 13
- 2.3   The Soul 20

3   Spiritual Evil: The Fatal Flaw in Liberalism   25
- 3.1   Pilgrimage to Europe 31
- 3.2   Kenya 38

4   Experiencing the Supernatural in the Bible   47
- 4.1   The Holy Spirit, Love and Spiritual Life 55
- 4.2   Spiritual Evil 61

5   Discovering Self-Deception   67

6   Discovering Mental Strongholds   77
- 6.1   Corporate Strongholds 82

7	**Discovering Father John**	**87**
	7.1 Wycliffe College	94
	7.2 Holland-Glenboro Parish	100
	7.3 The Gishler Group	104
	7.4 Interim Ministry in Alberta	106
8	**Developing a Spiritual Life**	**113**
	8.1 Community	117
	8.2 Orthodoxy	120
	8.3 Relevance	124
	8.4 Outreach	127

II	**Healing Spiritual Life**	**131**
9	**Wounds, Oppression, and Bondages/Strongholds**	**133**
10	**Healing Wounds From Trauma**	**139**
	10.1 The Birth, Life and Death of Mary	140
	10.2 My Slumbering Spirit	147
	10.3 Sexual Abuse	149
	10.4 The Spirit of Cancer	153
11	**Wounds from Personal or Inherited Sin-Guilt**	**155**
	11.1 The Law of Sowing and Reaping	155
	11.2 "Shrikeism" and Listening to the Holy Spirit	159
	11.3 Generational Sin	160
12	**Delivering Prisoners**	**165**
	12.1 Sexual Bondage and Alcoholism	166
	12.2 Homosexuality/Gender Confusion	168
	12.3 Masonic Oaths and Curses	171
	12.4 Identity Theft and Low Self-esteem	173
	12.5 Spirit of Slavery	176
	12.6 Spiritual Depression	177
13	**Exorcism: The Lost Gift of Christian Ministry**	**181**

14 Protecting Spiritual Life	187
Notes	197
Colophon	199

Foreword

This began as a love letter to my children. My objective was to warn them of the spiritual dangers of life on Earth and encourage them in seeking the love, joy and peace of an eternal spiritual life in Jesus Christ. As I poured out my heart, I realized that I also had many spiritual children who could benefit from the same wisdom. Finally I realized that since very few people had had the same traumatic experiences and learnings about the supernatural, this should become a public guide to discovering, developing and healing an authentic spiritual life.

Along the way I have been helped by many people. First of all my wife Lucille initiated my discovery of the Holy Spirit by giving me Catherine Marshall's classic book *Something More*. She has also given me the 38 years of love I needed to survive the emotional pain involved in these learnings.

The Rev. Canon Herbie O'Driscoll inspired me to learn to preach powerful sermons that help people in daily life. He also waded through my first attempt at serious writing and gave me valuable advice.

John L. and Paula Sandford had published their classics *Healing the Wounded Spirit* and *Transformation of the Inner Man* at just the right time to guide us in healing ministry in the 1980s. I was blessed by his reviewing the manuscript and offering wise advice.

My friends Marie Taylor and Jim Tubman stepped in to provide expert proofing and professional layout respectively. Mostly I have been guided by the Holy Spirit in discerning what is true and what is self-deception and delusional. Thanks be to God!

Part I
Going Spiritual

Chapter 1

Becoming Who You Were Meant to Be

We live in a time of spiritual confusion. Many people want to be spiritual — but not religious. They have been disappointed by religions and false teachers who promised to enrich their lives but left them confused. They are looking for something more. Something greater than and beyond the tangible worldly goals of sex, money, success and happiness. That something more, our spiritual life, is our intuitive relationship of love with God and all of God's creation — God the Father, Jesus, the Holy Spirit, other people and animals and the beauty of nature. It is something more because it includes both the physical and supernatural dimensions that most people cannot see in this life.

To understand our spiritual life we have to go back to the creation story in the Bible. Genesis 2.7 explains how the first man and woman were created. (Please let us not get sidetracked by religious arguments about creation here). The point is that, unlike the rest of creation which came into being because "God said, 'let there be'," men and women were uniquely formed by God out of the Earth when God breathed the breath of life (His Spirit) on them. Now you know why we have two overlapping circles on the cover. The bottom one represents our earthly body of flesh and blood. The top one represents our spiritual God connection, our personal spirit. As I was trying to explain this I glanced up at my wifi modem. This connects me invisibly to virtually every other computer on the planet. Our personal spirit, is our invisible intuitive connection to God the Father, Jesus, the Holy Spirit, other people and (bad news) Satan. The next chapter, Chapter 2 on page 9, will explain how the overlapping part of these two circles, our soul (our mind and will); acts as the "meat in the sandwich," managing the information from both the physical senses of our body and the intuitive senses of our spirit. Our spiritual life is essential to the quality of our physical or bodily life. It is the something more that enriches our daily life with love, joy, peace and meaning. *Going Spiritual* is the lifelong process of discovering, developing and healing a spiritual life, as we are transformed into completely spiritual beings. Our goal is to have richer lives of love, joy and peace — first on Earth and then in heaven.

Going Spiritual is a personal story of going from a young well-educated but naive liberal intellectual to the older and wiser Father John, who finally understands how things work in both the physical and supernatural dimension, and seeks to share his joy — and spare you the pain and suffering of discovering this the hard way.

My parents were both university graduates. My father had a Ph.D. in Chemical Engineering and we moved to Edmonton after 19 years at the National Research Council in Ottawa. He had his dream job. Design a research lab and hire about 20 Ph.D.s and technicians to develop new products for Chemcel. Many of the people that came to our house were university faculty so I grew up with a great respect for liberal intellectuals. Both of my parents had been emotionally traumatized by the loss of their mothers at an early age so I could only get their attention by talking about what was going on in national and international politics. Nobody believes me when I try to explain why I was never able to talk about my emotional life.

With my naïve liberal and intellectual background it was not easy to discover the truth about our human destiny. I was surrounded by many conflicting religious views and opinions about who God is and what God is trying to do on Earth. It was also the beginning of what has become a post-truth culture. The ideal of objective truth or what Dr. Francis Schaeffer called "true truth" has been discouraged by political pressure groups as possibly offensive to someone's human rights.[1] Schaeffer describes how the ideas of the philosopher Hegel

> "…led to the idea that truth can be sought in synthesis rather than anti-thesis. Instead of anti-thesis (that some things are true and their opposite untrue), truth and moral rightness will be found in the flow of history, a synthesis of them. This concept has not only won on the other side of the Iron Curtain: it has won on this side as well… our generation sees truth in terms of synthesis and not in absolutes. When this happens truth, as people had always thought of truth, has died."[2]

This flight from the possibility of establishing absolute truth has continued to our own time when "post-truth," as a description for our culture, was chosen by the editors of the Oxford English Dictionary as the new word of the year in 2016.

Like many people I had to learn how things work the hard way from the disasters of life. As I will share in Chapter 3 on page 25, the fear of growing up under the threat of nuclear incineration and war in the 1960s made me question why, if we are so smart, do things go so badly wrong in human history?

The pain of a divorce drove me to read the whole Bible, cry out to God and discover how things work in the supernatural dimension. Personal experiences of Jesus, the Holy Spirit, Satan and healing miracles made this dimension real. A job loss led me to discover how the human mind can deceive itself. It also led to the discovery of a new identity as Father John. The birth, life and death of our daughter Mary drove me to my knees in prayer and taught me to pray for healing and to love unconditionally. Finally, in reviewing the manuscript with my healing ministry mentor John L. Sandford I came to understand how mental strongholds blind people to the truth and are a major reason why things go wrong. Over the past 25 years of ordained ministry as an Anglican priest I have also learned what people need in a church community to discover, develop and heal their spiritual lives.

This profound learning has come at a terrible emotional cost. You cannot see all the scars now because my greatest spiritual learning has come from many experiences of guidance, blessing and inner healing from the Holy Spirit. Like most people I was very skeptical and needed to experience healing personally to really believe. The combination of head knowledge and personal experience opened my spiritual eyes so I could see and understand of how things work in the spiritual dimension. I would not wish any of these painful experiences on my children, or anyone else, so I am offering to share in practical detail what I have learned.

My experiences of spiritual discernment included the decision to write this spiritual autobiography for my children and grandchildren, to share my experiences and to warn them about false teachings. But first I needed to discern whether this was just my ego talking, or a genuine divine call to write. Judges 6.37-38 describes how Gideon tested the God's call on him to save his people from destruction:

> "Look, I will place a wool **fleece** on the threshing floor. If there is dew only on the **fleece** and all the ground is dry, then I will know that you will save Israel by my hand, as you said. And that is what happened. Gideon rose early the next day; he squeezed the **fleece** and wrung out the dew — a bowlful of water."

To do this myself I posed a question in prayer. I asked the Holy Spirit to give me a title for a book. It would have to be clearly not from my own mind or imagination. The response was a clear idea that formed in my head overnight. As I woke up, I intuitively knew the book title was to be in the form of an email heading. The email was to be a response to an email from an old friend. Rod had sent me an email saying that "we had differences." I knew he had lost his faith and would be very skeptical. He believed in science. Perhaps if I shared my own experiences of the Holy Spirit, spiritual evil and supernatural healings he would again be able to believe in the Jesus of the Bible. My thinking was that he might accept this as evidence that the supernatural worldview of the Bible was not a mythical exaggeration. He needed to know how I had been convinced of the authenticity of the supernatural worldview of the Bible. The heading for the email explaining all this that came to me, I believe from the Holy Spirit, was *Going Spiritual*. Enjoy!

Chapter 2

What is Spiritual Life?

We often use the words "soul" and "spirit" interchangeably with only a vague understanding of the difference. The difference is critical as many people confuse their emotional life with their spiritual life.

Watchman Nee, in his classic *The Spiritual Man*, teaches us that the soul and personal spirit are different in nature.[3] Nee spent a lifetime in prayer and study of the Bible for insights into personal spiritual life. Many people believe that we have a body which is our corporal or physical nature, and a soul which is our invisible spiritual nature. The Bible however, consistently refers to body, soul and spirit (1 Thess. 5.23, Heb. 4.2). The Biblical creation story (which is good science if you assume really long days) explains the relationship between body, soul and spirit. (Gen. 2.7) We are told God breathed "the breath of life" into his nostrils (body), and he became a "living soul". "The breath of life became man's spirit."[4] The soul is then the combination of this breath of life (passed on by inheritance), with a body to form a soul. The diagram shown in Figure 2.1 on the following page illustrates this relationship, showing the soul as the overlap or connection between the personal spirit and body. Understanding these relationships helps us understand how our spiritual life works and how sin, sexual pollution and identity confusion can be so destructive to spiritual life.

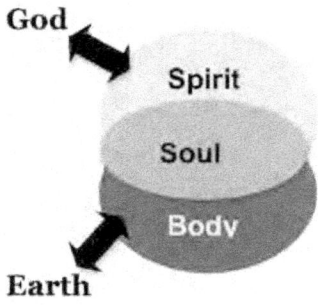

Figure 2.1: Body, Soul, and Spirit

Our spiritual life is the experience of our body, soul and spirit; connecting to God and other people in intuitive emotional relationships. These relationships can give us feelings of darkness or joy and peace. Our body soul and spirit are not separate identities. They are one entity with different functions as the eyes and ears have different functions. The consequence is that when anything goes wrong to upset this harmony all three parts may be affected. As we go spiritual we learn how this relationship works through the good and bad experiences in our lives.

2.1 Our Bodies:
(*Bios* — Biological life)

Our spiritual life is lived in and through our bodies. Our bodies connect us to the physical environment through our senses. Our bodies require food, water, heat and emotional relationship to survive. Our bodies have senses and feelings – touch, smell, hearing, seeing, love, fear etc. All this information is sensed by our body and passed on to our mind, which we think of as being in our soul. This information and our memory helps us stay alive in a physical environment that can be dangerous. In addition to this sensing information from our body, our mind also processes intuitive information from our personal spirit, the Holy Spirit and other people to make decisions and control how we move our bodies.

If we need food we sense hunger and act. Babies begin sensing the outside world in the womb. They seem to be able to pick up the emotions of their parents. They begin to wonder if this is a safe place. In a few cases babies in the womb — or even after birth — that have been completely deprived of love — seem to know that they are not wanted and have given up and died — for no obvious physical reason. Our bodies grow and develop physical and mental capacity. We begin to think and explore on day one. As we mature we begin to ask questions about why we are here. We also discover more needs and desires for safety, companionship, popularity and eventually sexual relationships. All the needs, wants and desires of our bodies pour into our mind (soul). This is where our priorities and actions are decided by our will.

Our bodies are the physical sensing part of our life. We sense pain when we stub our toe. We experience pleasure when we receive warm physical affection, taste good food or have a cold beer on a hot day. We see and appreciate the beauty of God's creation including other people with our eyes. When I sing songs of praise and thanksgiving to God, I have a physical experience of the supernatural dimension. I can feel the energy of joy in my upraised hands. This is sensed by my spirit as joy and also physically felt in my body. When I lay hands on a person and pray for healing, I sometimes see shaking or feel the warm glow of the Holy Spirit passing through me to heal someone. When I pray in tongues I know I have temporarily surrendered my voice to the Holy Spirit, who then prays through me to God for another person. These physical manifestations of the supernatural build up our faith and confirm the authenticity of the Biblical stories.

The Bible teaches us that our bodies are to be a temple for the Holy Spirit. "Do you not know that your bodies are temples of the Holy Spirit, who is in you, whom you have received from God? You are not your own; you were bought at a price. Therefore honour God with your bodies." (1 Corinthians 6.19-20)

The main function of our body is to be a sign of God's glory in the world; and to see, feel and appreciate His creation. We are to love God and enjoy God forever. This is what gives our lives meaning and purpose. This is why God created humanity. He delights in His creation. He desires to come and live inside us as the Holy Spirit. But the Holy Spirit cannot live in a body polluted by drugs, alcohol, overeating or a mind full of anger and bitterness. We become signs of God's glory in the world when we love ourselves, including our body, by not overeating. We are a sign of God's glory when we love and care for others. We are a sign of God's glory when we proclaim His good news of forgiveness and healing. We are a sign of God's glory when we take a visible and risky stand against lies, injustice, exploitation and any behaviour that is destructive to any part of God's creation.

Biblical teachings on the body have been distorted by false teachers who consider the body as inherently sinful and unholy. These teachings rob people of their true identity as beautiful and precious signs of God's glory in the world. This is the primary function of our bodies. Helping people recover their true identity as beautiful and precious children of God has been one of the most common and exciting parts of our healing ministry. The Genesis creation story describes the creation of men and women as "very good." (Genesis 1.31). It is an act of rebellion against God's revealed word, and thus a sin requiring repentance, confession and absolution; to believe God made a mistake or created an unwanted or bad person. The truth is that God created us as part of a world that is dangerous and gave us the freedom to make good or bad choices.

What many people do not seem to realize, is that this very good creation has been corrupted by human rebellion against God's authority. The Adam and Eve story (Genesis 3), explains how weak and foolish humans are tempted and deceived into this rebellion, by their own ego desires and by the work of Satan. While it may be the physical body that commits the sin, it is not the body but the heart or will that is ultimately responsible and becomes polluted with sin guilt. As we will discover, going spiritual is all about the transformational process of bringing our body, soul (will) and spirit into a deeper love relationship with our God, our self and our neighbour. Sadly, many people believe they can do this by being a good person. There is an excellent "Howard Storm in hell" video on YouTube[5] that will convince anyone who thinks they do not need Jesus for salvation, that they are in very big trouble.

2.2 The Personal Spirit:
God Consciousness

"*Zoe*" is the Greek word for "spirit life." We can think of our personal spirit as our intuitive connection to God, other people and all of creation. It is our "God consciousness." It is like our wireless connection to the Internet. We know it works, we depend on it, but do not really understand how it works.

Our intuitive intelligence develops as we get to the big questions of life. Is there something more than what we can see, hear, touch and smell? How did we get here? Why are we here? At some point we may become aware of another invisible dimension. Many people discover spiritual life in nature. The beauty of the natural world is so complicated, so incredibly well organized, that it could obviously not have just happened by accident. If there is a beautiful creation, there must be a beautiful creator, a "first-cause." Our experience of nature often turns our attention upward from the earth, to what people in most cultures have historically called "the creator," "god," or "the great spirit." This desire to connect with the divine creator is intuitive. Intuitive means we sense and know something in our personal spirit. We may not know in our rational mind — in the soul, where the idea came from.

Falling in love is a good example of intuitive thinking. I will be sharing the difference of trying to decide in my rational mind in our soul whether or not to marry — and getting it wrong, and many years later just knowing I was going to get married in my spirit in Chapter 4. Nicky Gumbel of Alpha Course fame uses the example of falling in love with his wife as what it is like to become a serious, Holy Spirit-filled Christian. When you think or feel you may be in love (with your mind), you probably are not. When you know for sure that you are in love intuitively (with your spirit), there is no doubt. Intuitive knowing is often more reliable than as rational thinking.

Our spirit differs from our soul which processes information rationally through our mind, will and emotions. People who have a "slumbering spirit" (see Chapter 10) often have a narcissistic "soul life," which is all about them. They may be confusing this with a spiritual life which is all about being in an intuitive communion/communication/relationship with God, nature, self and other people. Notice what Mary says in the Bible when she finds she is pregnant with the long-promised Saviour: "And Mary said: my **soul** (mind) glorifies the Lord and my **spirit** rejoices in God my Saviour" (Luke 1.46-47)

Many people in our "post-truth" time are seriously misguided in discounting the Bible writers as "pre-scientific" thinkers. In fact they had a much better understanding of how things work in the invisible spiritual dimension. Mary understands rationally in her mind (soul), and her personal spirit is intuitively filled with joy. She intuitively knows that what the angel has just told her is both physically impossible and yet true. She responds to this intuitive knowledge by giving glory to God for honouring her as the mother of Jesus. This is an example of intuition (personal spirit) over-riding rational (mind/soul) analysis and thinking to comprehend truth. A modern practical example of this is that men who have a less developed sense of intuition often miss emotional signals and intuitive information and get into communication problems with women who are naturally more intuitive.

The most common experience people have of this intuitive/personal spirit knowledge, is their conscience. Most people are aware of a general feeling of badness or guilt when they have done something seriously wrong. They may not ever be caught or forced to face what they have done; but somewhere deep down inside they have a dark feeling. In their soul (mind) they may be trying to justify or cover this up as winning; but in their heart (spirit) they intuitively sense something is wrong. This is the decision point where each of us has to chose between ignoring these warnings and dealing with them. If we choose to ignore these warnings we are missing an opportunity to go spiritual, and allowing our personal spirit to become more and more polluted by sin-guilt. If this approach is continued, our spirit may become so polluted that it withers and is unable to maintain our communication link to the divine.

If we have invited the Holy Spirit into our lives in Baptism: He may also have to leave and return to God if our personal spirit becomes too polluted with sin-guilt. The holy cannot live with the unholy on a spiritual garbage dump. Ultimately, like Eve, our spirit may become so polluted and weakened that it dies and cannot carry our soul to heaven when our body dies. This is the point of the misunderstanding between Eve and Satan in the Fall Story (Genesis Chapter 3). Satan deceives her by telling her she will not die. She assumes (wrongly) that it is talking about physical death and that she will continue to live with God in paradise. Satan knows she will not die physically, but she will die spiritually in her love relationship with God through disobedience (failure to love). She and her descendants (that's us) are put out of paradise to suffer through our physical life until our weakened personal spirit cannot keep our physical body alive.

The Good News of Christianity is that God made a New Covenant through the sacrificial death of Jesus, to enable the forgiveness of the sin that pollutes human spirits. Many people have trouble with the idea of a man (Jesus) dying for the sins of the whole world. But Jesus was not just a man, because God Himself, not Joseph, was His biological Father. (Matthew 1.20)

Our personal spirit is our connection to the supernatural dimension; we need to listen to the Bible with our intuition as well as our mind. This means interpreting the text of Bible very carefully and intuitively, assuming that Jesus is who He said he was — "God's one and **only** Son, who is himself God and is in closest relationship with the Father...". (John 1.18) The rest of us are children by adoption. The key point here is that while Jesus the human man could not give his life as a ransom to God for the sins of all men; the life of Jesus as the only fully human and fully divine Son of God; would be an appropriate sacrifice. It does all hang together logically if we can get our spiritual eyes opened and expand our rational human thinking. It has also been very helpful to me to generally assume that in the Bible stories, Jesus is almost always using everyday physical things and experiences to help us understand this spiritual dimension and how we relate to it.

This spiritual or intuitive sense of the goodness or badness of choices has also helped me in making important decisions. My best illustration of this will be my two stories of deciding on a marriage partner shared in detail below. My first decision to marry, which was based more on intellectual analysis — the old "she loves me, she loves me not" problem — ended in a painful divorce. The second decision which was based almost entirely on spiritual intuition and a dramatic sign from the Holy Spirit; it has led to 38 years of love, joy and peace. This is why counsellors often advise people to "follow their heart" (spirit) in deciding intuitively which way to go — which I did the second time.

Intuition also helps us find good friends and avoid people who are spiritually destructive. It took me a long time to learn how to listen to my spirit. Now I can talk to someone for a few minutes and know whether or not we are on the same spiritual page.

Our personal spirit is not the same as the Holy Spirit. If a person becomes a serious Christian believer as a result of Bible reading, religious instruction or a personal experience of the divine, they can ask Jesus to send the Holy Spirit to live inside their personal spirit. We know this "living in" is not a mistranslation. The earliest Greek texts of the Bible have a dative case, which means physically inside. I will share my own dramatic experience of the Holy Spirit, which is called being "born again" or "baptized in the Holy Spirit" below. This was the point where I started developing a much deeper Christian spiritual life as my spirit was nurtured and healed by charismatic worship and experiences of supernatural healing.

Our spiritual life changes dramatically when we begin to understand and personally experience the Holy Spirit. The Holy Spirit offers us spiritual gifts which transform us, opening up our spiritual eyes so we can see things and understand things that we could not see and understand before. Most people know about the gifts of love, joy and peace. The spiritual gift of love is far more powerful and wonderful than the emotional lusts of our mind in the soul. The spiritual gift of joy is a much more powerful experience than the emotion of happiness. Peace, specifically peace with Jesus and those around us, is far more profound than the emotional state of not being in conflict or feeling anger. I have learned to recognize people who have a serious spiritual life. They have light in their eyes and sometimes actually glow with the Holy Spirit. In contrast many of the people around us may have muddy eyes and appear to be unhappy, sad or even angry. This Holy Spirit glow is the origin of the halos around pictures and icons of holy men and women.

The Holy Spirit is also our teacher, guide, healer and comforter. As I grew deeper in my spiritual experiences and learning (not just by reading books), my conscience grew stronger and I began to get "words of knowledge." This is how prophecy works and explains the divine authorship and consistency of the Bible. I will share the context of my divorce decision below but it was actually a word of knowledge on a bus travelling between Edmonton and Calgary that convinced me divorce was the right decision. I was praying for wisdom and heard in my head the words "It is better to bite the bullet and loose a few teeth than to die slowly of lead poisoning." In the context I took this as divine permission. In case you are suspicious, this was a year before I met Lucille.

The intuitive nature of our spirit is enhanced by the Holy Spirit gifts of knowledge, wisdom and prophecy. One of the most practical things I learned was how to get my 300 lb. sailboat on top of my car. In a dream the Holy Spirit showed me a video of me tipping the boat on end, balancing it on the middle of the car rack, then lifting the bottom end up (by myself) and pivoting the boat around to rest on top of the car.

Even more helpful have been the many times when I was desperately searching for a sermon theme that would bring the chosen readings together. Without fail, as I prayed and read the passages again, a new idea would form in my head of what the "Spirit is saying to the church." This is what we mean by the divine inspiration of the Bible. If you doubt this, read Isaiah which was written 800 years before Jesus (or better yet the whole Old Testament). Compare this with the Gospels and you will notice that the God described in each book is essentially identical. This is how dozens of authors, who lived hundreds of miles and centuries apart, could describe the same God. My experience in Bible study has been to notice things I did not remember seeing before. My spirit was coming alive and adding to the mental capacity of my mind and soul. This is the essence of *Going Spiritual*. Your spirit life must dominate your soul life in the mind and will. If the worldly desires and lusts of the body dominate the mind and will, this can lead to rebellion against the divine will, sin and spiritual pollution.

The most practical teaching on the functions of our personal spirit was published in John and Paula Sandfords' *Healing the Wounded Spirit*.[6] They identify nine specific functions of the personal spirit. These functions help us understand how our spirit enriches our life and transforms us into "signs of God's glory in the world":

- To worship God in spirit and in truth.
- To have satisfying personal devotions.
- To hear the voice of God in dreams, visions, intuitive hunches and sometimes aurally.
- To give us inspiration and creative ideas.
- To enable us to transcend time and see the future consequences of present actions.
- To transcend space and connect to people intuitively.
- To experience the glory of the married sexual union.
- To protect the body from disease.
- To act as a good conscience.

I learned most of what I know about the personal spirit from the Sandfords. Their two classics on healing spiritual life — *Transformation of the Inner Man* and *Healing the Wounded Spirit* — were published in 1984 and 1985. This was when we were desperate for information on healing prayer after our daughter Mary was born. Their teachings on how to nurture the personal spirit coincided with the dark warning of the medical team that finally let Mary come home. They called us in and said, "There is nothing more we can do. If the love of the family does not help Mary grow she is on the way to the end."

The Sandfords taught us that the personal spirit of a baby "…needs to be met, welcomed and nurtured through warm physical affection."[7] John Sandford also shared how the warm family fellowship that he grew up in nurtured his spirit and provided a community where he also learned to cherish his own person. This was not an unhealthy narcissism, but a healthy self-love — as in the commandment to love our neighbour as well as we love ourselves.

Since our spirit is our connection to God, it is also nourished by our participation in public worship and daily devotions. Worship and earnest prayer is like establishing an internet connection or connecting a pipe through which the Holy Spirit can flow into our spirit and nourish it. Sandford describes the Holy Spirit as the "…power of our life…"[8]

The most powerful experience of spiritual nurture is participation in Holy Communion or the Eucharist (celebration). This includes worship singing, Bible reading and teaching, beauty in liturgy and music, confession and absolution of sin, blessing prayer and an opportunity to renew our baptismal covenant and reconnect with Jesus. Lucille and I began our first days of ministry in Manitoba with a daily Eucharist or Morning Prayer service in the church. We continue to read scripture and pray together first thing every morning and last thing at night.

Finally, the Sandfords note that our spirits are nourished by Christian reading, classical music and the beauty of nature, poetry and art.

Unfortunately, many people (myself included), are tempted to turn on the TV and pollute their spirits with the ocean of pornography, violence and secular thinking that passes as entertainment and news. This pollution flows into our minds and pollutes our spirit and our soul. *Going Spiritual* requires an intentional choice to nourish, develop and heal our personal spirit.

2.3 The Soul:
Self Consciousness

The original Greek Bible uses a different word for the soul: "*psyche.*" This is the root word chosen for the academic discipline of psychology. Psychology is a relatively new academic discipline that has added to our ability to diagnose and treat mental illness through behaviour modification techniques and drugs. It has also, sadly, replaced most of the pastoral counselling and spiritual direction work historically done by priests. While psychology can advise on behavioural dysfunctions and treat chemical imbalances in the brain, psychologists are often not aware of the diagnostic gifts and healing power of the Holy Spirit. Only Christian psychologists would be aware of the healing power of the self-examination, repentance, confession and absolution process explained in Chapter 11.

Our soul is our personality and our identity. This is what makes us a unique human being. We go spiritual or fail to go spiritual depending on which voice dominates our soul. Our body, soul and spirit all need to be "born again"/transformed or healed so we can be made whole, holy and survive in heaven after our spirit can no longer keep our body alive.

The soul includes our emotions — the essence of our life. This is how we become fully alive and experience other people and the world around us. Our emotions enrich us (happiness) and also protect us and warn us of dangers around us (fear). Our emotions are our response to information from the physical senses of our body (touch, hunger, physical danger, beauty etc.). They are also a response to intuitive information from our spirit (love, joy, peace). Our mind processes sensing information from our body as well as intuitive information from our spirit. Our eyes tell us what a person looks like on the outside and our spirit (intuition) tells us something about their spirit and soul. One of the things I learned from experience is that men tend to have a less developed emotional intelligence than women. Couples in marriage counselling often spend a great deal of time learning to communicate emotionally as opposed to rationally. Our emotional life is so important that healthy well-fed newborn babies have been known to simply give up and die if denied warm loving affection.

While the body, soul and spirit are one and the same physical entity, the diagram will help us understand how the soul is like the meat in the sandwich, between our personal spirit above and our body below. The soul includes our mind (CPU in computer terms), memory (hard drive), will (programmable software) and emotions. The soul is our identity and self-consciousness — connected in the diagram in Figure 2.2 to both our personal spirit above and to our physical senses below. The arrows illustrate the function of our soul, specifically our will, in arbitrating among the sometimes conflicting desires of our spirit and body.

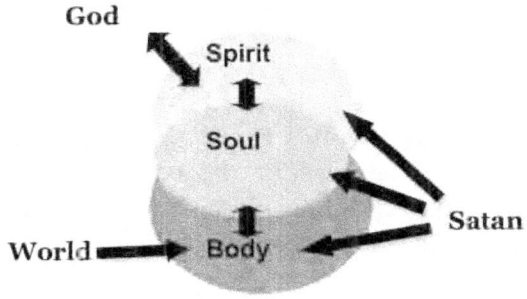

Figure 2.2: Spiritual Conflict

Our soul is our mind, memory, emotions and will — the history and essence of who we are. The soul is our unique identity as a human being. It is the invisible part of us that Christians believe receives a new heavenly body when our earthly body dies — and lives eternally with God, in another dimension called Heaven. In Figure 2.2 on the preceding page, the soul is the overlapping communication link between the body and personal spirit. The arrows help us understand why spiritual life is a struggle. From our body the mind and soul receives constant worldly demands to prioritize physical and emotional comfort and pleasure. It is too hot, too cold, hungry, sad, lonely, fearful, etc. From the other side (top) the soul receives opposing demands from our spirit to prioritize love, joy, peace etc. The spirit, soul and body may also be deceived by Satan into wanting more than we need or things that are destructive. This can lead to the sins of pride, lust, gluttony and covetousness.

The Holy Spirit as the voice of God in our spirit is also constantly guiding us through our spirit. God does not try to control our lives. God loves us and wants a personal relationship of love with us. To accomplish this He has had to give us free will to accept or reject that love. This is very dangerous. Real love is always dangerous. The good news is that God has provided us with detailed instructions for a life of joy in the Bible. He has also promised that believers will receive the gifts of the Holy Spirit to guide them and, when we fail, a way to be forgiven and restored to relationship. Figure 2.2 on the previous page shows both God and Satan contending for our loyalty.

The question is always, "which side are we listening to and letting dominate our will (soul)?" For example we have minds and bodies that may be telling our soul that we need alcohol or a sexual experience. Our soul (mind) may not be listening to the voice of our spirit warning that this is may be spiritually dangerous. Our spirit may intuitively know the danger, and be saying "no." The soul is in the middle of our personal spiritual struggle. Depending on which voice is dominant; the soul will either say "no" to self-destructive behaviour, or say "yes" and slip into spiritual separation and pollution. Each choice strengthens the domination of one side or the other. These are the choices we make or not make wisely in developing our spiritual life.

Finally and critically, the soul includes our will or volition. The will is the part of the soul that arbitrates between all the intuitive information of the spirit and the sensing/experience of the body. There is a constant but invisible battle between the holy desires of the spirit and the sometimes unholy desires of the body and mind for control of the will. Whichever side controls the will, ends up in control of the body and mind. The will is where we sort out truth, priorities and direction in our lives. Our will or volition decides on our values or priorities. These values or priorities change over time, as our will learns from experience. Everything we learn from past decisions and experiences influences our will in developing new values and priorities for our lives. It is not unlike updating the software on a computer as problems are found. Our spiritual life grows stronger or declines, depending on the choices our soul makes.

The good news is that we are not alone. God has never stopped reaching out to His creation in love. Our lives seem to consist of a number of experiences, challenges and disasters which seem to almost be designed to get our attention. This is of course dangerous. God is taking a risk here as many people give up the search for spiritual life. They may think that if God loved them He would not let bad things happen to them. This is common, tragic and wrong. The opposite is true. God is testing us. Hardship and suffering test our love. Do we really love God, or are we only spiritual dabblers, unwilling to be totally consumed by the fire of God's love? All the great spiritual masters — Abraham, Moses, Jesus, John the Baptist, Paul, Mother Theresa, etc. — suffered ridicule, hardship, beating and many even death. If I had known all the hardships I would suffer, I might have given up myself. This is written to save my children and grandchildren from some of the pain I have suffered in discovering a joyful spiritual life. So let me encourage you to stick with the work of *Going spiritual*. It really is the best thing you will ever do in this life. It's worth it!

Chapter 3

Spiritual Evil:

The Fatal Flaw in Liberalism

Looking back, it is clear that God tried to get my attention for a long time by focussing it on the big question of "why do things go wrong?" If God is love and all-powerful why does God let bad things — really bad things like war, genocide and disasters — happen? The philosophical problem is the apparent contradiction in believing that God cannot be either all-loving or all-powerful if He does not prevent some of the really terrible things that happen.

Many people lose their personal faith — or give up on God at this point. Looking back from old age and experience, I can now see that the better answer is to expand our understanding of both "all loving" and what God is doing in the long run. "All loving" needs to be expanded to infinity — beyond our earthly lives and into the heavenly or spiritual dimension. If we can get this, we can begin to understand how extremely important we are to God. We can begin to understand how God desires to test our love, and then strengthen and re-test it with something even harder to grow our love. Our love relationship with God and His creation — particularly our self and our neighbour — is the essence of our spiritual life.

It might help to see *Going Spiritual* as the like of body building. People lift heavier and heavier weights as they grow in physical strength. Let me share some of the harder challenges in my life, as examples of how God has guided, tested and helped me discover a deeper and richer spiritual life of joy through ever harder tests of my love and loyalty.

When I was born in Rouyn-Noranda, Quebec in 1942, the world was a dark place. Germany had invaded Belgium, France, Austria and Poland. The British Expeditionary Force in Europe had been pushed back into the sea and evacuated. My father was working as a chemical engineer at a huge gold mine in Quebec. We soon moved to Ottawa where he settled into a nineteen-year career with the National Research Council. A whole series of traumatic events focussed me on the question of why things go wrong. The first was when my beloved dog Nicky had to be put down because he bit some old lady at the kindergarten. I was about five and distraught with grief. My take on this was that the old lady probably deserved to be bitten. I learned early that life is not always fair. Next my dog Toby was run over by a car. This was my first experience of witnessing a death. It was bloody and messy. I learned that life is messy, dangerous and temporary.

My next lesson in "things going wrong" was in a childhood deception and betrayal that helped me discover the central lie in "progressive" and "liberal" thinking. I was about ten and had just spent three weeks building a fairly elaborate tree-house in Ottawa from scrap wood. My friend Jim said he had a better idea and offered to help me build it. First we had to dismantle my new tree-house. I still remember the grin on his face after we had taken my beautiful construction down. He told me he did not have a better idea. He was just jealous. I learned a powerful lesson in human betrayal and deception. I am reminded of this almost daily when I read of new "progressive" ideas in the church and society that promised a better life for all. The problem is that we have to trust them and give up the old way of thinking (that we know works) in order to try a new way that may or may not work. This experience taught me that the reasons why things go wrong include human weakness, selfishness, jealousy, deception and the struggle for power.

The fifties were an idyllic time to grow up. The men had come home from the horror of the Second World (1939-45) determined to have a happy family life. Rebuilding produced prosperity so more people could afford a house. Building housing produced more employment and more homes that exploded into more suburban living. Walt Disney spread the Christian values of love, honesty, kindness and truth through happy movies and then the new medium of TV. (Yes, Grandpa grew up before there were TVs and computers.) It was still a bit like an idealized historic Christendom when men and women knew who they were, feared God and went to church. People who were sexually confused kept it to themselves. People felt secure that there was a God in Heaven and were happier. Looking back this was a little like my tree house. It was beautiful and it worked.

Things began to change in the sixties. There was a general sense of rebellion against all forms of authority. The First World War had revealed the incompetence of generals (men) and governments (men). Women's liberation was at its height, as women demanded admission to all professions — including government, the military and the clergy. Next there was sexual liberation. The invention of an effective birth control pill meant that sexual activity could be separated from the consequence of responsibility for children and a long-term relationship. Looking back, it was as if the "tree house" of the way the world worked in the 1950s was being slowly dismantled. The old order of church, government and families, where men and women knew their roles, was being dismantled. Secular humanism, individualism and liberal theology was replacing the old order of Christendom.

The rebellion against authority included the mainline Christian churches. Academics in liberal democracies have questioned and challenged the authenticity and divine inspiration of the biblical text and the authority of the Church since the Enlightenment. Academics and many Christian clergy now misunderstand the supernatural spiritual worldview of the Bible as largely mythical. Jesus is now understood by many church attendees as a good teacher —

but not a necessarily a divine saviour and miracle worker (as in the Bible). Many baptized Christians (including me at the time) have not read the whole Bible or experienced the Holy Spirit. They do not know or understand how the supernatural spiritual dimension operates, and how it can affect their lives. They do not really believe in Satan or the danger of evil spirits that can test, tempt, torment and destroy the creatures of God. Many more liberal clergy have abandoned the historic sin — redemption theology of the Bible as too harsh.

Discovering the reality of Satan and spiritual evil in my life, helped me enormously in understanding why things go wrong. It was the missing piece that explains why basically good and intelligent people do things that are not just foolish and destructive, but evil. Evil is destruction with no redeeming benefit. The attempt at destroying the Jewish race during the Holocaust, for example, can have no redeeming purpose. It was also focussed on God's chosen people. Having ruled out all the other rational explanations for this particular "thing going wrong" — I was forced to look beyond the natural to the supernatural.

The biblical worldview of a deceiving spiritual force of evil is actually a much better and a more coherent and scientifically verifiable explanation of why things go wrong than the new progressive/liberal explanations of a disadvantaged childhood, bad choice, or ignorance. This has been probably the most important learning of my life.

Cowboy movies and "playing guns" were my favourite form of recreation as a child growing up in Ottawa. One day, I challenged all eight kids on my city block to a gunfight. We started from opposite ends of the street but they were hopeless. The last two survivors were standing under a tree trying to figure out where I was. They neglected to look up.

The movie *Shane* had a very powerful impact on me. This is a classic 1950s (good) farmers vs. (bad) ranchers Western. The big rancher hires five professional gunfighters to terrorize and discourage the farmers (sodbusters) from fencing off parts of the open range into plowed fields for their crops. The rancher drives his cattle through the farmer's fences and fields. Tragedy strikes when one of the farmers' sons becomes frustrated, straps on a gun, and goes into town to get himself killed in a hopeless gunfight. Shane is a mysterious stranger who has been recently hired by one of the farming families as a labourer. Hidden in the bottom of his bag is a very professional looking gun belt which he puts on as the families are in grief over the killing. Shane rides into town and kills all five gunfighters and the rancher in a spectacular gunfight.

This movie became a motivating vision for me. I was very naive so *Shane* taught me that there are some really bad people in the world — people that you probably can't just persuade, shame or educate into behaving nicely (as liberalism assumes). I found potential purpose and meaning for my life in the apparent need for a gunfighter or someone who had very special skills to be able to help protect people from bullies. Yes this was a grandiose saviour complex. It has motivated me to get from where I was (intellectual liberal), to where I am now (*Going Spiritual*). While I am terrible on a shooting range, I have developed the more powerful skills of writing, teaching, healing prayer and spiritual warfare in the name of Jesus and under the guidance of the Holy Spirit. As modern priests try to help people in their relationship with God and each other, they are not unlike Shane and the ancient prophets, who lived dangerously in challenging the local rulers when they had displeased God or abused their subjects. My ministry as an Interim priest for twenty years was much gentler but sometimes not unlike that of Shane, in confronting and bringing God's love and healing to destructive individuals in churches.

My family moved to Edmonton in 1954 where my Dad had been appointed Director of Research at Chemcell. We attended Holy Trinity Anglican Church where I became President of the Anglican Young People's Association and had some brief but powerful experiences in planning and leading youth services. My parents were shocked by the friends I made in High School so I was sent to what is now St. Michael's University School in Victoria for grades ten and eleven. This taught me to find meaning and purpose in mental discipline and physical fitness. The school motto was "A sound mind in a sound body." The regular hour of Physical Education every day taught me self-discipline. Fond memories include coming in the top ten in our weekly 4.5 mile run, carrying a rugger ball over the goal line in a mud puddle and playing soccer in three inches of snow. There was also a daily chapel time where we sang hymns and had a Bible reading before announcements. The words of these hymns and the Bible must have penetrated to my soul and nourished my long process of *Going Spiritual*.

The wider questions of why things go wrong became more important to me at the University of Alberta (1962-1965). The 1960s were an exciting time to be a university student. Young people were challenging government and all forms of authority. It was the height of the Cold War. NORAD was ready to launch an all out nuclear war on fifteen minutes notice. Canadian and American pilots slept in bunkers beside their nuclear armed planes with engines on on at the end of runways in Germany. They could be airborne in four minutes — the time they would have before Russian incoming missiles struck. I remember walking to University during the Cuban Missile Crisis in 1962, and watching the sky for a mushroom shaped cloud. My Army Militia training during high school had included terrifying pictures of nuclear bomb tests, showing in slow motion how a typical city street with houses full of dummies would be blown away by the blast, incinerated by the heat and poisoned by the radiation — from ten miles away. There was a "ban the bomb" group — Combined University Campaign for Nuclear Disarmament which I joined and soon became the President. This included leading a large public demonstration down Jasper Avenue in Edmonton. I am on the right carrying the sign in the photo. We were protesting Canada accepting nuclear warheads for our ill-fated Bomarc missiles.

This issue began my career as an activist letter writer. This included a letter to Prime Minister John Diefenbaker about the Avro Arrow cancellation. Designed and built in Canada by Canadians,

Figure 3.1: Nuclear Protest.

was clocked by the Americans in slight climb at 1,200 MPH — a record speed in the late 1950s. This re-enforced my determination to understand why things go wrong and that human fallibility was part — but only part — of the answer. There was something still missing from my naive liberal intellectual understanding of why things go wrong.

3.1 Pilgrimage to Europe:
Evil Up Close

When I graduated from the University of Alberta with my B.A. in Economics in 1965, there was an opportunity to spend eight weeks in England and Europe. The Student Union chartered a flight for $300.00 that would drop us off at Gatwick Airport, near London and pick us up eight weeks later. It was an amazing adventure that started and ended in a Youth Hostel in London. In between was a whirlwind tour of London, then north to Coventry and Edinburgh. I went west to Loch Lomond and then Holy Loch in Scotland. Holy Loch is not on the tourist maps. It is a very deep fjord on the West coast of Scotland and was the home base of the US Polaris and Trident nuclear submarine fleet. This was the heart of the US deterrent against a surprise nuclear attack. At that time each submarine carried 24 intercontinental ballistic missiles. These could be launched underwater and target any city or military facility in the world, with a nuclear warhead that would kill almost everyone within a twenty to fifty mile radius, depending on wind patterns. Each submarine could do more damage than was done by all the explosives of both sides in both World Wars. And who did I see crewing and guarding these submarines — eighteen-year old American Marines. I discovered how dangerous and fragile a place the world of the 1960s was.

Like many others in the sixties I was trying to understand evil — why bad things happen to good people, and why people and nations seem to do such destructive and irrational things. The threat of nuclear incineration and human extinction focused our minds on the failures of past generations and into a questioning of authority — particularly political and religious authority. What I did not know was that the Holy Spirit was very gently drawing me into intellectual and emotional relationship with God and what humans had done to God's good creation.

My European trip was more a religious pilgrimage to experience military sites and graveyards, than the usual European fluff tour of famous places. The real purpose was to engage emotionally with the problem of evil in history. After a very brief circle through Larne in Northern Ireland and Dublin, I was back in London to ditch the 26 lb. suitcase, and travel even lighter through France, Spain, Italy, Austria, Germany, Belgium and back to Gatwick.

My next lesson in human evil was Dieppe in France. In the dark and desperate days of World War II, the Canadians had been chosen to attempt a "raid" — on German occupied France. The Russians were bearing the whole weight of the German Army and had been pushing the Allies to invade occupied France and open a new front. The Dieppe Raid was a test of attacking and landing soldiers and tanks on a fortified and well defended French beach. Dieppe was a spectacularly poor choice. Tragic experience revealed that the diameter of the pebbles on the beach below the town did not give tanks enough traction to climb over the sea wall and open a path for the 1,200 Canadians pinned down on the beach.

Figure 3.2: Dieppe Raid Bunker.

The British planning and execution was a disaster. First the Air Force found themselves unable to provide air cover. Then the Navy withdrew from providing offshore covering fire from battleships and finally the only radio that seemed to be working was carried by the only three soldiers, who got over the seawall, ran across a field into the town and radioed back "we (not only three of the 600 of us) are in the town." This led to the assumption of success in the command ship offshore. Because the radios were not working they did not know the other 600+ soldiers were pinned down on the beach and being slaughtered. A second wave of troops was landed to join the 600 others trapped on the beach under relentless fire from hidden bunkers.

Figure 3.3: One of many French WWI cemeteries.

It was a powerful experience to look down from the hidden German bunkers and notice that there was not a mark of them. There were about 300 Canadian graves and the rest had been forced to surrender and spent the war in captivity. Sixty years later I was serving as Interim Priest in Olds, Alberta, and was honoured to lead a memorial service for the surviving veterans of the Alberta Tanks. The only good news was that this probably saved thousands of lives later, in the D-Day landings further South. This disaster raised doubts in my mind about my naive liberal assumption of the infallibility of reason and education in governing human activity.

Of course I had to visit Paris and see the Eiffel Tower, Louvre, L'Arc de Triumph, Versailles and Notre Dame Cathedral. The latter was particularly interesting as there was a sense of the holy there. Then it was back to the grim world of the First World War in France with a visit to Verdun, north east of Paris. This is where both sides were determined to prevail at all costs — including the lives of over a million men on each side. I could not get to Fort Duamount because there was no traffic going that way and it rains every fifteen minutes. This is apparently normal and helped me understand the suffering of the soldiers living and dying in mud filled trenches. The scale of the conflict is indicated by the graves and the dozen huge vaults at the fort containing body parts. The graves are a real monument to an evil beyond human folly. I was being guided to look for something more than human weakness and ignorance at work in the world.

After a wonderful time visiting the tourist sites in Barcelona and Madrid, I continued hitch-hiking back through Marseilles, Monaco and Florence, then north to Innsbruck in Austria and Germany. My interest was on what had happened at Nuremberg. This was the location of the most famous Nazi political rally and the War Crimes trials after the Second World War. The Nurnberg Courthouse is not on the usual tourist route. They were incredibly helpful and considerate. An official reached in a drawer, took out a file of old black and white photos and walked me down a long series of corridors to the actual courtroom used in 1946. He explained some renovations and showed me the photos of where the most infamous Nazi officers and officials had sat and where the judges had sat. Forty-five years later I was standing inside a gas chamber at Mauthousen concentration camp in Austria. By then I understood evil as both human weakness and spiritual oppression from my own experience.

The most dramatic day of my life was probably the day I went through Checkpoint Charlie into East Berlin (see photos of the wall (Figure 3.4 on the following page) and entrance (Figure 3.5 on page 37)). At the time the monstrous Berlin Wall completely encircled the part of the city still occupied by England, France and the US. Access was through about 100 km of East Germany, occupied by a Communist government. An eight foot high wall, topped with glass and barb wire ran right through the heart of the city (see Figure 3.4 on the following page).

Figure 3.4: At Berlin Wall, 1965.

Tension was high during the Cold War. Hundreds of residents from the East had tried to escape by climbing over, tunnelling under or even taking balloons over at night. Many had been killed by the Russian soldiers patrolling the 100 metre "no-man's land" on the East German side. An American tank was stationed at Checkpoint Charlie, one of the main crossings.

They briefed me on the Western side and told me to be very careful who I talked to and what I said. Passport in hand I walked (slowly — because if you run they shoot you), through the gate and presented myself at the eastern side. They also asked me questions and told me to be careful. The eastern part of Berlin was a dramatic contrast to the western. Virtually no restoration and rebuilding had taken place in the twenty years since the war had ended. It was drab and sad with little in the shops and no people bustling about. I have a photo of this deserted main street. As in Paris I got talking to a man and he invited me to his flat for private (possibly) conversation. Life was very hard. This was punishment by the Russians who had lost millions of soldiers and civilians in the War.

Coming back through the Berlin Wall was a moment one never

Figure 3.5: Checkpoint Charlie Approach.

forgets. They warned again, to walk slowly across the 100 metre open space to the exit guarded by armed Russian soldiers. I took my passport and walked very slowly across. It was really clear to me that if they did not want you to go across, you would not be able to go across. For the first time in my life I was a real captive. It was a great relief to be back in the West. This was a powerful lesson in the fear and the evil of control.

What happened there thirty years later was also a powerful lesson in overcoming the power of spiritual evil. A few elderly women came out of a church one night with lighted candles to pray near the Wall. The next week a few more people came out at night with lighted candles and joined them. Eventually the crowds grew so enormous, that when the Communist leaders looked out at the thousands of candles lighting up the city they realized they were no longer in control. Next the soldiers ignored some young men who started breaking a hole in the Wall. The love of God had once again triumphed over the power of evil and fear!

The men who led the "Great Powers" into two world wars were not fools and not ignorant of history. The answer of "human weakness, deception and ignorance" to the question of "why is there so much evil in the world?" seemed inadequate to explain what had happened. My sense was that there must be something more. There must be another, deeper, root cause of the evil things that happened in history. It took me another fifteen years and the trauma of a divorce that drove me to the Bible to discover this hidden answer. I discovered the reality of Satan and evil spirits, or spiritual evil, as the "something more," the hidden cause of why things going wrong. This was an essential part of my experience of *Going Spiritual*. It exposed the consequences (millions of lives lost) of the liberal intellectuals deconstruction of the supernatural world view of the Bible and intellectual blindness to the reality of spiritual evil in deceiving world leaders.

This discovery of spiritual evil was re-enforced by a wonderful meeting with John Sandford at age 88, to help me edit the manuscript. He shared the background story of how he had done a workshop of healing corporate strongholds (see Chapter 8 on page 113 in Germany after the war. Pastor Berthold Becker attended his workshop and he took these teachings on organizing nation-wide prayer against the corporate stronghold of war and aggression back to East Germany. This is how the ladies with the candles had defeated the power of Satan over the German people.

3.2 Kenya:
Spiritual Values Trump Economics

The 1960s were also a time of "de-colonialism." The British Empire was disintegrating as local politicians in India, Africa and Asia came to London to demand independence. Colonialism was very politically incorrect. It had associations with racism, slavery and intolerance. But there were consequences. The biggest consequences of sudden independence was corrupt government and economic development practices. My motivation for studying Economics was to find meaning and purpose for my life by helping people in these newly independent countries. They did not have enough locally trained teachers, engineers, agriculturists and doctors. There was a fantastic opportunity to do something really worthwhile — and gain experience and travel.

As I was graduating with my B.A. in 1965, an idealistic group of recent graduates were working with Canadian Universities and the Federal Government to establish the Canadian University Service Overseas. This would become a recruitment agency which would work with newly independent governments in Africa, Asia and South America, to place recent Canadian graduates for two years in local government positions. Many of the first CUSO Volunteers served as teachers. If you had a B.A., you could teach up to High School — with 3 weeks intensive teacher training in Canada. Other volunteers went overseas as Agriculture Officers, Doctors and Lawyers. One of these doctors later shared a frightening story of removing an arrow from someone's head. In Canada he would have had to wait ten years to get that kind of experience.

Before going to Kenya I had a very important decision to make. Throughout my trip to Europe I was wrestling with the question of whether or not to marry Claudia. We had been dating, taking the same political science and French classes and enjoyed each other's company. She had also applied to CUSO and been placed in South America. I was placed in Kenya. When I got back to Canada from Europe we would only have ten days before leaving for CUSO Orientation in Toronto. We had to either get married now and change the placements; or wait two years to see each other. I had a very low emotional IQ, as I realized much later; and was trying to decide rationally what to do while travelling in Europe. When I returned to Edmonton we were still both unsure. After three days together, I proposed and we scrambled to put a very small family wedding together in one week. It was to be fifteen years later that I learned that if you are not sure you are in love, then you are not in love. It is wiser to wait until you are sure.

CUSO was still scrambling to find a second placement for my new wife in Kenya as we headed East for orientation. We had three weeks of teacher training and a two week overseas cultural orientation in Montreal. This included a visit to the Centre for Tropical Diseases and instruction in using our heavy duty emergency medicine kit. Transportation overseas was provided by the Canadian Air Force and included landing at the infamous Entebbe Airport, where Israeli commandos had recently rescued Israeli hostages in a huge fire fight. There were still bullet holes in the terminal building as we landed to drop off the Uganda CUSO volunteers. We were the first 15 CUSO Volunteers to arrive in Kenya, which had been independent from Britain for only three years in 1965.

On arrival we were met by the Deputy Head Master of Menengai Secondary School in Nakuru. It was supper time, so he took us for dinner with some relatives in Nairobi. It would be a two hour the trip down into the famous Rift Valley to Nakuru. Mr Patel and his family were part of the large Asian community that made up the middle class of Kenya at that time. The Asians had been brought over from India to construct the strategically critical East African Railway because of their experience. This linked British controlled Mombasa with Uganda and Lake Victoria. So there we were on our first evening in Kenya, surrounded by unbelievably hot curry dishes with the strict warnings of our Tropical Diseases orientation to never drink the water. Sweat was pouring down our faces but we did not drink the water.

This got even funnier when late at night in our hotel room in Nakuru, we decided it was time to break out the water purification tablets. First of all we had to get past the mosquito netting to even get out of bed. We soon learned this netting was just for the tourists, as Nakuru is higher than mosquitoes can fly. Anyhow, out came the emergency medical kit with its huge bottle of water purification tablets. Dissolve, wait ten minutes, then drink. Ugh! The next day when

Figure 3.6: Assembly at Menengai High School.

I asked about the water at the Hotel desk I was told (in a very British accent) "Good Lord man, you can drink the water — the British were here!"

The next day we set off (on foot because CUSO volunteers are encouraged to travel like local people), to find the Principal of Nakuru Secondary School. This was the other high school, where we were told Claudia was to teach. It was a Saturday, so of course we found the Principal in a bar. He had of course had heard nothing from the Ministry of Education in Nairobi about a new CUSO teacher from Canada, but he was delighted to have another teacher, and guided us through weeks of paperwork to "make it so." We spent a whole day in Nairobi, two hours away, walking the required documents from one office to another in the Ministry of Education, and waiting for all the right approvals. They were very good to us. We learned that the "Africanization" of the government was not just bringing local people into former colonial positions. It really meant the "Brotherization" of employment opportunities. Senior officials hired their relatives (whom they could trust) as opposed to the most qualified applicant in a competitive process. Their tribal value of loyalty was stronger than their self-sacrificial value of Christian love. This is a critical flaw in academic economic development theory which often ignores cultural values.

It was some time before I made the connection that if religious and cultural values drive politics, and politics drive economic development, then the most important thing we can do to facilitate economic development and overcome poverty is tell people about God's grace, love, forgiveness and healing. The missionaries were actually doing more for the people than all the billions of dollars in of foreign aid. God was meeting me where I was and leading me into the process of *Going Spiritual*.

One of the classic books on economic development, Tawny's *Religion and The Rise of Capitalism*, teaches this historic link between Protestant Christian cultures and successful economic development. Some people don't like to hear this but it is true. Ask yourself what is the dominant historical religion in the ten wealthiest countries. Like England during the Industrial Revolution, people needed to have a belief in and fear of God to overcome their fear and self-interest, and adopt the Christian values of self-sacrificial love and trust. Kenya had been blessed with Christian missionaries who are still establishing and maintaining schools, orphanages and laying the foundation for a prosperous future fifty years later.

Kenya was an amazing experience. We lived first in a house with our own cook/housekeeper, Linus. He would stand at the door on the way out and firmly remind me each day of what he needed in the way of supplies. We grew very fond of Linus and were invited to visit with him and stay overnight in a real thatched roof hut. It was near Lake Victoria and very clean and cool. Our adventures included driving all around Kenya, Uganda and Tanzania with a flight to Zanzibar. I was teaching East African History and Geography so it was interesting to see Murchison Falls, the headwaters of the Nile. We also saw the Anglican Cathedral on Zanzibar, the site of the original slave market. The smell of cloves covers the whole island. We also visited Olduvai Gorge in Tanzania, where Mary Leakey had found the oldest fully human skull, before "Lucy" was found in Ethiopia. We saw the famous Archeologist Louis Leakey, at the hotel bar on our first night.

Figure 3.7: Flamingo Lake.

Nakuru is named after the nearby lake which is famous for the thousands of pink flamingos. (See Figure 3.7.) The lake is very shallow, so there is a natural cycle of the flamingos' droppings fertilizing the plants, growing in the water, that becomes their food. There are millions of them, so that as we arrived in our car and walked toward the lake they would start taking off, but only the ones at the edge had room to fly. Fifteen minutes later they were still taking off. There were all kinds of other birds there, including giant pelicans with a six foot wingspan.

Just north of town was Menengai Caldera (see Figure 3.8 on the next page). It was seven miles across and I took my students on a

Figure 3.8: Menengai Caldera.

field trip inside to see the lava flows. Canadians should be embarrassed to hear that my Form 4 (grade 12) students were learning physical Geography that I had learned at university. They would know how a caldera is formed when the middle part of a volcano falls in. Claudia was a geology major and so we led a small group of members of the East African Geological Society on a tour inside the caldera.

We also went on a safari to climb an active volcano. Ol Doinyo Lengai began spewing small amounts of ash while we were in Kenya. It was near the Tanzanian border, so we had to go with a group that had a land rover as there were no real roads, only dirt tracks. We got about half way up, camped overnight then realized the ridge we were on ended and had to turn back (see photo of me with pack on slope). Along the way we saw lots of game, particularly giraffes.

Figure 3.9: Camping on Oi Donyo Lengai, Tanzania.

On another trip we were in a game park where I was able to take a picture of 14 lions from the open roof of a vehicle. There were no bars between us. Serengeti is the world's largest caldera, a collapsed volcano with steep sides preventing animals from escaping. There is one narrow road down. Then you just drive around with the animals.

My take-away was a feeling that I had gotten far more out of the experience than the people of Kenya. I was able to make a meaningful difference in the lives of our students and the local people we got to know and love. In addition to two years of teaching High School Geography, History and Physical Education, we established a 4,000 book school library. I led a Scout bus trip to see Baden Powell's grave on Mt. Kenya. I spent one four week vacation teaching local teachers the entire high school Geography syllabus. One of the high points (!) was climbing Mt. Kenya and getting through the snow to the lowest of its three peaks. This took two days going up and one day coming back. These experiences enriched and added meaning and purpose to my life.

Chapter 4

Experiencing the Supernatural in the Bible

Coming back to Canada after two years was a shock. I had grown used to being surrounded by poverty and talking to coloured people. Montreal seemed very white and affluent in comparison. My first shopping trip was hilarious. I had grown so used to bargaining over prices in Kenya, that I just automatically expressed mock outrage when some poor employee in Eaton's told me a pencil cost ten cents. Correspondence with McGill University about their Centre for Economic Development indicated this could lead to a career path for me as an Economist. I showed up a week before classes were due to start and by grace and persistence managed to get accepted for an undergraduate makeup year doing five courses including statistics.

Claudia was pregnant and our son Christopher was born right in the middle of my final exams at McGill. There is something very special about becoming a father. It adds meaning and purpose to life and teaches self-sacrificial love. You are suddenly responsible for a helpless baby that is totally dependent on you. A couple becomes a family. They have a living, breathing and growing sign of their love relationship. It is a wonderful opportunity to grow in love as you play and do things together.

Academically, McGill was a disaster. Imagine a very average B student, who has been teaching High School for two years in Kenya, suddenly in the Fourth Year Honours Economics class with the best and the brightest students in Canada. You can see that this was not going to end well. I was so busy studying I never even saw the McGill Centre for Economic Development, the reason we were there. What I did not know at the time, was that God was using my desire to help people through economics, to draw me to His even better plan of helping people discover, develop and heal their spiritual lives.

Our young family moved back to Edmonton, where all of Christopher's grandparents parents lived for a career reboot. I found three very interesting temporary jobs and discovered my gifts. The key event in this time was some testing in employment skills at the University of Alberta. The Counsellor who examined my scores turned to me and said "You are good with people, good at organizing things and have worked in a library; have you ever thought of becoming a librarian?" I had. But had also rejected the idea. Now, In view of the test scores, it seemed to make sense. We moved to London Ontario in September 1969.

The School of Library and Information Science at the University of Western Ontario is modelled on the Harvard Business School and teaching is based exclusively on student-led seminars. There were no lectures. It was perfect for me. Each seminar was led by a team of four students who had to research and jointly lead a one hour discussion on a topic like "the literature of physics." What does it include? How is this information organized and accessed? Each student would have to hand in two sheets of paper the day before the seminar. One page indicating what they had read and the other summarizing what they had learned.

It was a wonderful education that has served me well for over 40 years working as a Librarian, Records Management Consultant and Interim Priest. One of my big "learnings" at the School of Library and Information Science was that people lie when completing research surveys. My master's thesis was a survey to discover how graduate students at the University of Western Ontario go about finding books, magazine articles and other information in libraries. This was pre-Google so the options were a card catalogue of books by author and subject, magazine and journal indexes published monthly, newspaper clipping files and specialized reference books. We asked our sample of students a lot of questions including a few to test for honesty and integrity. For example we discovered a significant number of graduate students, who claimed to have used the non-existent library resource *Poetry Abstracts* to find information. This was both amusing and sobering.

My career as a professional Librarian gave me meaning and purpose. My first professional library job was as Administrative Assistant to the Chief Librarian at The University of Western Ontario. Dr. Robert E. Lee was a real Southern gentleman who gave me wise insight into people and Library management. Soon there was a vacancy as Business Librarian in the famous Richard Ivey School of Business Administration. This was perfect, as I was very interested in management.

Computers were a new thing. It was important for students to find current information on specific companies, industries and individuals. The best sources were the Globe and Mail's *Report on Business* and the *Financial Post*. I was soon on the leading edge (bleeding edge) of computerization and developed the Biz-News Index. This was the first computer generated index to the Globe and Mail. My first email was sent in 1971.

We continued to live in the married student residence in London Ontario as Claudia was working full time on her Masters Degree in Geology. I was working hard at the Business Library and did not realize our marriage was in serious trouble, until she suggested we have a trial separation and go for counselling. The counselling helped me realize how out of touch I was emotionally. We had a reconciliation after a few months and got back together as a family in London, Ontario.

I had met the director of the Calgary Public Library at the Canadian Library Association conference in Toronto and been invited to

49

apply for a management position. I applied a few months after our reconciliation and was offered the position. We agreed to all move to Calgary, with me going ahead in September and Claudia to follow a few months later when her Master's degree was completed.

I was very busy settling into my new position in Calgary. We did not phone often and I noticed that we did not seem to really miss each other. When she came to Calgary for the Library Staff Christmas Party, then flew off to Edmonton without staying over, I realized that the relationship was over.

We had not been attending a church regularly during our eleven years of marriage but divorce seemed unacceptable to me on biblical grounds. It would take me another year of prayer and working through the biblical teachings on love, divorce and forgiveness; to finally resolve this. This crisis of conscience is what drove me to read the whole Bible — as opposed to just isolated quotations out of context. The most relevant quotations (out of context) are:

- "For this reason a man will leave his father and mother and be united to his wife, and the two will become one flesh. So they are no longer two, but one flesh. Therefore what God has joined together, let no one separate." (Matthew 19.5-6)
- "I tell you that anyone who divorces his wife, except for sexual immorality, and marries another woman commits adultery." (Matthew 19.9)
- "This is my blood of the covenant, which is poured out for many for the **forgiveness of sins**." (Matthew 28.26)
- "He went into all the country around the Jordan, preaching a baptism of repentance for the forgiveness of sins." (Luke 3.3)
- "...and repentance for the forgiveness of sins will be preached in his name to all nations, beginning at Jerusalem." (Luke 24.47)
- "Peter replied, 'Repent and be baptized, every one of you, in the name of Jesus Christ for the forgiveness **of** your sins. And you will receive the gift of the Holy Spirit.'" (Acts 2.38)
- "All the prophets testify about him that everyone who believes in him receives forgiveness of sins through his name."

(Acts 10.43)
- "In him we have redemption through his blood, the forgiveness of sins, in accordance with the riches of God's grace." (Ephesians 1.7)

In order to really understand and trust Jesus' teachings I found I needed to get to know Jesus personally, rather than as an ideal model of behaviour. What I discovered was a heart of holiness and love, radiating compassion and grace. Jesus is always reaching out to sinners with the offer of forgiveness. There is no limit to either the number of times or the depth of sin. The grace is free but dependant on three conditions.

1. There must be genuine heartfelt repentance. This means exposing and dying emotionally to the attractive power of the sin.

2. God has made forgiveness conditional on both repentance and personal belief that Jesus could give up His life on the Cross for that sin.

3. Forgiveness depends on asking Jesus for forgiveness and our accepting this forgiveness from Him. He can not intervene without our specific permission.

I had gone through years of agonizing over the seriousness of the marriage covenant, starting during our separation in London. I could still remember the priest wrapping his stole around our joined hands and saying "Those whom God has joined together let no man put asunder."[9] We had shared wonderful experiences together in Kenya, Montreal and London. We had a beautiful child growing up and enriching our lives. We had similar interests and lively discussions. But something was missing. It was not anybody's fault.

It was also very important to me that I was not dating other women and was doing this on the assumption that I might never marry again. The Church of England has a very wise rule that you cannot be married in the Church to the person responsible for your divorce (i.e., Charles and Camilla).

As I pondered this on a bus between Edmonton and Calgary I had a revelation. It was what is called a word of knowledge, probably from the Holy Spirit. The words that formed in my head were "It is better to bite the bullet and lose a few teeth than die slowly of lead poisoning." Later on, while reading my way through the Bible, I came to the realization that God loved me like a father and would forgive me for making a mistake and for breaking my marriage vows. This would be conditional on my being genuinely penitent, going with faith in Jesus to confession with a priest and providing for the family.

Meanwhile I was finding my new job at the Calgary Public Library very absorbing. As a Department Head supervising three professional librarians and three support staff, I was responsible for selecting reference and circulating books and magazines. Librarians were the pre-internet and pre-google way of finding information. Reference librarians (like Lucille in the photo) sat at desks in the public area of the library surrounded by a special collection of reference books in a particular subject area. They answered any factual question from either people in the library or by phone.

The development of on-line computer searching provided a better alternative to monthly paper indexes to magazine articles. I also worked with IT staff at the University of Alberta to develop an experimental computerized index to Government documents — Caldoc.

Having accepted the reality of my marriage breakdown and the probability of divorce, I settled in to what I call my year of "hermiting." A wise friend pointed out the danger of newly separated men getting emotionally involved with women, before they have figured out who they were. When you are married it is sometimes difficult to separate out who you really are.

I made two key decisions. First, I decided to commit to a year of not getting emotionally involved with women while I tried to sort out my new life. I would go on group hikes and to social events but

Figure 4.1: Lucille on the reference desk, 1977.

not get into dating.

The other key decision was to use this time to read the Bible (all of it). My ex-brother-in-law, the Rev. Bob Arril, had given me a Bible for Christmas years before. Like most people I had not actually read it. Now there was a need to know, not just about divorce, but about what God really wanted and what Jesus had actually taught. I developed a discipline of reading the Bible every night before bed. This became a habit. Even if tired or if it was very late I would still read the Bible for a few minutes before going to sleep. My years at boarding school in Victoria had taught me self-discipline. It took over a year to get through the Bible from beginning to end. That did not matter. It was so interesting and believable that I was hooked. I was being drawn into an exciting intellectual and spiritual relationship with the divine. It was the key step in going seriously spiritual. I started out by reading the whole Bible story. Then I began to believe and experience the Bible story. Now I have begun to live it and become part of the Bible story myself.

This reading led to first understanding, and then to experiences of and belief in, the supernatural worldview of the Bible. My spirit began to connect to God's Spirit. As I started to personally experience the love, joy and peace of the Holy Spirit, I moved from "knowing about it" in my head, to "knowing in my heart" (spirit), that the biblical accounts of supernatural prophecy, healing miracles and the resurrection of Jesus are authentic historical accounts. This personal experience of the supernatural makes it much easier to go from knowing about, to being a believer in. This is why most modern charismatic and Pentecostal churches are flourishing, while more traditional churches that avoid "emotional" teaching and experiences of the Holy Spirit are dying.

Regular Bible Study, prayer, Christian fellowship and developing a personal emotional relationship with Jesus and the Holy Spirit is essential to the process of *Going Spiritual* as we will see in Chapter 8 on page 113. This process goes on until the day we die and our life continues in new, transformed spiritual body and we have gone completely Reading the Bible daily, is critical to the process of discovering, developing and healing a spiritual life.

One of my earliest mentors was Dr. Peter Craigie. He lectured in the Religious Studies Department at the University of Calgary, was active in Cursillo and offered courses at our annual Theology Alive Conferences. His Deuteronomy course and commentary, the *Book of Deuteronomy*, helped me understand the importance of law in Old Testament Theology. God (the real God) is a God of order. Order is a component of holiness which is perhaps the primary aspect of God's nature. This is in sharp contrast to modern liberal theology, which tends to downplay law, order and holiness and focus almost entirely on love as inclusion. As we will see in Chapter 9 on page 133 on healing, I discovered that the interpretation of sin in the supernatural dimension is extremely legalistic and specific. Sadly many people and clergy in our time do not accept the authority of Old Testament teachings as equal to New Testament teachings. The consistency of descriptions of God as holy (complete) creator of order between biblical texts written during the Babylonian Captivity (500 years before Jesus) and those written by Paul (sixty years after the death of Jesus) are evidence of a single divine source as the author or one who inspired all the writers of the Bible.

4.1 Experiencing The Holy Spirit, Love and Spiritual Life

Daily Bible reading is addictive. Our personal spirit rejoices when the truth is spoken. By my second time through the Bible (I had just kept going), I began to notice more and more references to the Holy Spirit. This was another thing I did not seem to get much teaching on in church. This is probably because the original Greek word (wind or breath of God) was badly translated into English as "Holy Ghost" in the King James version of the Bible and Anglican *Book of Common Prayer* (1962). It is tragic that many modern people have given up on Christianity and gone to Hinduism, Buddhism and new age cults for personal (but counterfeit) spiritual experiences and teaching. The discovery of the Holy Spirit as the authentic ongoing presence of God in my life, has been my most important learning.

People who have not read the whole Bible carefully might easily assume that the Holy Spirit first shows up as a dove (John 1.32) at Jesus's Baptism by John. Others might assume the Holy Spirit showed up at Pentecost when tongues of fire came down on the Apostles (Acts 2.3) and they began speaking in foreign languages. Closer study reveals that it was the Spirit of God (Genesis 1.2), that hovered over the waters of chaos in the very first paragraph of the Bible. One of the greatest rewards of reading the whole Bible, as opposed to selected passages, is that we begin to see how central the Holy Spirit is to what God is trying to accomplish in reaching out to us.

The story of my relationship with Lucille begins with a job interview in the library over a year after I realized my marriage was over. My Supervisor and I were hiring a Reference Librarian. We interviewed some candidates and found one young woman particularly suited. She had the academic and experience qualifications, and we sensed she would be very good in dealing with the public. I felt myself drawn to her in a strange way. My Supervisor and I agreed she would be the best candidate. Later, walking home to my apartment, I noticed her on the other side of the street but thought it unwise to tell her the good news. This was very fortunate. At the same time as our interview, another librarian in the Cataloguing Department was having an emotional melt down. She needed to be moved to another department. As a union member she had the first right of refusal on vacant professional positions and was transferred to my department.

A few months later our first choice candidate, Lucille, was interviewed by the Head of the Business and Science Department and offered a position. Over the next few months we met occasionally over coffee and had lunch. We both sensed an attraction. It was like I had known her before, so we explored our life histories without finding any link. In order to have more time for this, I invited her for dinner in my apartment. I made beef stroganoff for dinner. We had a nice bottle of red wine and talked on my balcony as the sun set over the Rocky Mountains. Much later, as she left to go home, I heard myself say, "I love you" as she left. Lucille replied, "I feel the same way" as the door closed.

There I was, having just told someone I loved her! I was already separated and going through the divorce process but still legally married. What was I going to do? Open the door and say "sorry it was just the wine talking"? I did not know what to do next. I sat down in my chair, threw up my hands and prayed this really sophisticated prayer: "HELP!!" It was actually more like "HELP NOW!!"

For what seemed like about the next half-hour as I sat in my chair, it felt like being under a warm water fall. An invisible warm energy just poured over me and poured over me and poured over me. I was bathed in love and joy and peace. It was what some call the baptism of the Holy Spirit. At the end of this, I said something profound like — "I'll take that as a yes." The Holy Spirit had become real to me. I knew where to go for the truth. The other half of the story, is that Lucille went home and phoned her two good friends and told them she had just met the man she was going to marry.

A huge take-away for me from my experience was that when you are really in love, you know for sure that you are really in love. This was in sharp contrast to the confusion and doubt in my first decision to marry. From that dramatic moment on, there was never any doubt that we would get married, and have a wonderful marriage. This experience of Holy Spirit-based wisdom has also helped me in counselling many couples.

Lucille and I had to wait for almost two years to sort out the painful details of a divorce. This was before "joint custody" of children, so sadly, conflict arose like a dark, heavy cloud of anger. It descended on what should have been the best years of all of our lives. I had proposed that Christopher come and live with me in Calgary when he had to change schools for high school, but decided to give up when the lawyer said a custody battle would cost at least $50,000 with only a 50/50 chance of success and be very emotionally destructive for everyone.

The good news is that thirty years later Claudia and I had a huge reconciliation. She had married a wonderful man and had a good marriage for many years. When my precious daughter Mary died in 2009 Claudia sent a condolence card that finally broke my heart. It moved me to thank her for her kindness and ask her to forgive me for the damage I had done to her heart. She replied and forgave me, lifting the veil of un-forgiveness that had been hanging like a dark cloud over both of our lives for 30 years. For us at least, the cloud finally lifted. Unforgiveness is a terrible burden, an emotional prison and a sin that pollutes our spiritual life. As we will see in Chapter 9 on page 133, un-forgiveness is the most destructive and common sin that we encountered in thirty years of healing ministry.

Lucille and I had a long courtship as the divorce process worked itself out. Lucille was way ahead of me spiritually. Her parents had served as missionaries with the China Inland Mission from 1934-1944. Their house was bombed by the Japanese and they had to flee to India. Her father Cliff Paulson has started the Christian and Missionary Alliance Church in Innisfail. Every day her father conducted evening devotions around the supper table. Scripture was read without comment and prayers were said.

One of the things that impressed me about Lucille was her determination to find the truth about God. She was raised on endless Bible meetings in a strict evangelical environment. She knew intuitively (her spirit) that something was missing from their teaching and fellowship. Later on in High School in Saskatoon, she became involved as a student with Inter-varsity Christian Fellowship. She discovered what she was missing — the love of God. This was a huge discovery for both of us. While evangelical churches tend to be more Bible based, many tend to over-focus on the Bible as a rule book for good moral living. As we will see in Chapter 7 on page 87, evangelical Christians often develop a rich spiritual life based on outreach and orthodoxy, but are starved for lack of real love, intimacy and emotional community. In contrast the more liberal Christians develop a spiritual life rich in love and community, but impoverished and weakened by a lack of deep orthodox biblical teaching. This over-emphasis on either biblical law or love is the basis of the current split in many Christian churches. I was deeply impressed that Lucille had persisted in going on from her very conservative evangelical upbringing, to explore Anglican, Baptist and Presbyterian churches.

It was on a train travelling in Europe that Lucille had read the classic Catherine Marshall book *Something More*. This book tells the story of how an experience of the Holy Spirit had brought comfort and healing. Catherine Marshall had already experienced the Holy Spirit in a Presbyterian church, but not really understood what was going on. Lucille, who like me had never had any teaching on the Holy Spirit, was asking the same questions as Catherine Marshall.

Was her faith lacking? Did she have some secret sin-guilt? Prayer did not seem to help. In the desperation of a long and painful depression, Catherine Marshall had been so desperate that she turned her face to the wall and cried out to God to either heal her or take her life. The result was a dramatic warming experience of the Holy Spirit. She knew God loved her. She knew God was with her, and that she was not alone. This is the same book that Lucille quietly gave me as a present before we were married. It opened up my spiritual life like a light switch in a dark room.

When Lucille and I were married in 1979, a Charismatic renewal was sweeping through Christian churches in Alberta. We attended Holy Spirit conferences in Calgary led by Rita and Dennis Bennett and Michael Harper. In addition to the teaching, which was new to us; we had an opportunity to hear people singing in tongues, praying in tongues and giving prophecy. There was also an opportunity to have prayer for physical healing, emotional healing and spiritual healing. During one workshop I was freed from an evil spirit, that I had inherited from my father. I was also "slain in the Spirit" and experienced the peace and joy of "resting in the Spirit." I simply fell semi-conscious, backwards into the arms of waiting "catchers." It was close to my experience of the Holy Spirit as a warm shower as I rested on the floor in the love, joy and peace of the Holy Spirit. This lasted for about ten minutes and was a wonderful experience. This renewal gradually faded out in most Anglican Churches in Canada. There was one very dramatic exception later at a large Diocesan Conference at the Banff Centre. The Holy Spirit suddenly and visibly swept through the audience like a wave, with several people weeping and slumping down.

This loss of awareness of the Holy Spirit has been a crippling impoverishment for Christian believers and spiritual life in many churches. While we often claim to be in Holy Spirit-led-churches and pray for guidance; many Christians are not aware of having a clear personal experience of the Holy Spirit. Since all baptized believers are promised they will receive the Holy Spirit as a sign of inclusion in the Heavenly Kingdom, I have always focussed my preaching on the gifts of the Holy Spirit and how they help us discover and develop our personal ministry in a parish church. (John 20.22, Acts 1.8, 8.15)

For example:

- **Words of knowledge or wisdom** — receiving a helpful idea or a phrase forming in your conscious mind that helps in preparing sermons or finding keys.
- **Faith** — intuitively knowing something is true, like Jesus resurrection and Mary knowing God is the father of her baby and that He is the Messiah.
- **Healing** — physical, emotional or spiritual healing through the work of the Holy Spirit as explained in Chapter 8 on page 113.
- **Miracles** — unexpected events like healing, forgiveness, grace and people calling at exactly the right time.
- **Prophecy** — intuitively receiving a word of knowledge or message that is to be shared. For example, after an Anglican Church Synod that had just affirmed the sanctity and integrity of same-sex marriage, a friend had the prophecy: "I will no longer listen to the prayers of this church." Clergy need this gift (and courage) to preach effectively.
- **Distinguishing between spirits** — little voices discerned in our heads, that prompt us to do good or evil. A spirit of joy or love (from the Holy Spirit) will make us feel good. A spirit of anger or confusion (from Satan) will lead us in a destructive direction that is contrary to biblical teaching.
- **Tongues/Interpreting Tongues** — speaking or praying in a language you do not know through the guidance of the Holy Spirit. An interpretation should be given except when praying in tongues.
- **Leading, Teaching, Encouraging, Giving, Serving and Mercy** — less dramatic but essential gifts to be discovered and used by those who have them for the benefit of the community, as each person finds meaning, purpose and joy in their spiritual life (see Romans 12.6).

Going Spiritual is a long gradual process of experiencing these gifts of the Holy Spirit which guide us in our lives, convict us of our sin, and heal, energise and comfort us when things go wrong. As we discover and experience the Holy Spirit and the spiritual dimension our lives are enriched, healed and made joyful!

Many churches unfortunately avoid teaching about the Holy Spirit because this is controversial. Not everyone receives the same gifts. This has historically led to spiritual pride, judgement, conflict and even church splits. It is tragic that God's plan, that people receive different gifts deliberately so they depend on each other in a community which has all the gifts; becomes corrupted and destructive through human pride and fear. Even more embarrassing, is the fact that many clergy have never had a powerful experience of the Holy Spirit. Personal experience moves our understanding of — and our belief in — the Holy Spirit, to a new level of certainty and depth.

There is a sad gulf of faith between those I would call "spiritual people" (who have had a personal experience of the spiritual dimension), and those who have not, and are what I would describe as "religious people" (who have not had such an experience). Religious people tend to focus on liturgy, ritual and doctrine — the tangible. Spiritual people tend to focus more on intuition (their spirit), personal experience and emotions. Modern clergy are generally trained academically in universities. We are given the pompous and possibly blasphemous degree of Master of Divinity, when in fact many of us have very little "mastery" (experience and understanding) of the third member of the Divine Trinity.

4.2 Spiritual Evil:
Swimming in the Deep Water

My mentor Canon Herbie O'Driscoll made an interesting comment on my *Seven Great Deceptions* manuscript. He noted I was swimming in the deep waters of spiritual life by talking about spiritual evil.

Figure 4.2: Deep Waters.

Since then I have gone much deeper in experiencing how Satan talks to people, deceives them into sin and then accuses them of sin before God. This is dangerous territory — like scuba diving. It seemed appropriate to share a photo of me as a certified diver, 60 feet under the Caribbean off Mexico coming over a coral reef (Figure 4.2).

The question in my mind, walking through European war cemeteries back in 1965, had been, "Why do things go so destructively wrong in this world?" A new answer came to me dramatically and powerfully. Lucille and I were dating secretly at the Calgary Public Library. We both worked on the same floor but in different departments. As I was a department head and in management, it seemed best to keep our relationship private; at least until my long-delayed divorce was finalized. We would leave the Library separately, meet up a few blocks away and then go to my place, her place or out for dinner.

So there I was standing on a busy street corner in downtown Calgary, beside the woman I loved. As we waited for the light to change, I was noticing the huge volume of cars and trucks rushing past us in the chaos known as rush hour. A thought quietly formed in my mind. "You could just push her a little and she would fall into the traffic and be killed and nobody would know."

I broke out in a cold sweat. Where the hell was this coming from! How could I hurt the woman I loved? Then the truth dawned like a bright light. We are not alone! Satan, whom the Bible teaches was the angel of light before he rebelled against God and was cast out of Heaven to the Earth, really does try to deceive people by whispering lies in their ears! This was one of my most profound experiences.

I had clearly experienced the voice of spiritual evil. This made the stories of Job, Jesus temptation by Satan and Jesus casting out demons real to me. This is where reading through the whole Bible pays off. Personal experience of the supernatural in our time confirms the supernatural worldview of the Bible. Personal experience moved my faith to a new and deeper level. My experience of the supernatural opened my (intuitive) spiritual eyes, to see the truth.

This is often a challenge. It can divide us from those who have not had personal experiences, and cannot believe in spiritual forces of evil. Discussing our supernatural healing experiences is critical to helping non-believers understand and begin to accept the truth of the Bible. The challenge is to do this without offending and creating conflict in families that can drive those we love away from discovering their spiritual life.

I had the sad experience of being told that while I was preaching and sharing my experiences of healing ministry at an ordination, my former bishop was visibly rolling his eyes behind my back. Many Protestant clergy are taught theology by academics who have not had experiences of the supernatural. They tend to be theologically liberal, and dismiss the books of the Old Testament as essentially mythical pre-scientific Jewish history. For example instead of seeing the story of Job as a deep theological teaching on how God can use evil, they ignore the Satan part at the beginning and use the story to teach how not to comfort people in emotional and physical pain. Job's friends all assume poor Job has done something bad and deserved his punishment. They miss the deeper teaching that God is testing Job to increase Job's faith. The wrong assumption is that Job is being punished by God for sin. Instead of (falsely) repenting and asking for forgiveness as his friends urge, Job cries out to God for justice. Job has a real love relationship with God. He loves God enough to challenge God.

What Job does not know — and most people seem to miss — is the first part of the story. The story begins with a theologically profound conversation between God and Satan. Satan is asking God for **permission** to afflict Job and test his love of God. This teaches us that Satan is under the authority of God. Job gets it right by faith. He challenges God's justice, survives, and is completely restored with his wife and more children and livestock.

I am sharing this because I have seen so many people who have lost their faith when life became difficult and God did not seem to be there to help them. The good news is that when these people do experience healing prayer they rediscover their faith in a God who does in fact love them deeply.

Lucille and I learned about demons and exorcism from experience. This seems to be the only way. Many Protestant clergy do not really believe in serious oppression by evil spirits. Those who do have some experience are often afraid to talk about this in their sermons because it is so controversial. Vague sermons about the love of Jesus are safer. They keep congregations ignorant but happy. This is sad because instead of people learning about and experiencing supernatural healing in Christian churches, they get distorted and wrong information from popular books and movies.

With the exception of original movie *The Exorcist* — which is a grossly exaggerated true story — many movies reduce the spiritual battle with Satan to a struggle between good and evil people. Instead of clergy having a central place as the good guys in protecting people from evil, they are often portrayed as the bad guys. The author Dan Brown for example, regularly denies the authenticity of the Bible, and ends up helping Satan obscure the consequences of Jesus' sacrificial death on the Cross. For example he ends one of his wildly popular movies with his idea of a secret very spiritual looking biological descendent of Jesus Christ — which challenges the authenticity of the Bible. Most of the millions of people who see these movies never hear the more exciting good news of supernatural healing and spiritual protection in churches. Many people have learned to dismiss Christianity and the church as having nothing to say about how things work in the supernatural dimension. This is exactly what Satan wants. How can people protect themselves against an invisible enemy they and their religious teachers do not understand or believe in?

People of the Lie, M. Scott Peck's story of discovering evil and the limitations of psychology, also convinced me of the reality of spiritual evil. Dr. Peck was a highly trained psychiatrist who had a challenge. He worked with a woman for four years, trying all of the psycho-analytic techniques known. Nothing was working. In spite of being an atheist at the time he sensed (spiritually) and came to believe that this woman was basically evil. While she discontinued therapy before he could suggest exorcism, he later began working with teams of psychiatrists and clergy in long (three day) and very stressful and dramatic exorcisms.[10] This was certainly not "best practice" as we will see in Chapter 13 on page 181. The point was that he had been an atheist, and became a serious Christian as a result of these experiences. He went on to write more best-selling books and speak at Christian conferences.

My first experience of deliverance from spiritual oppression (exorcism) was not quite as dramatic. We were at a healing conference in Calgary with a visiting Anglican priest from Borneo. After the conference, there was an opportunity for personal prayer so I went up with a number of other people. I did not have a specific problem in mind but was aware of my not having a good relationship with my late father. The priest went along a line and when he prayed over me in tongues I began to shake. Then I fell backward into the waiting arms of two strong men. They laid me gently on the carpet — beside all the others who had been "slain in the spirit." I "rested in the spirit' for a while. then got up realizing that something was different. I felt lighter. I talked to the priest. He explained that he had cast out a spirit connecting me to my father in an unhealthy way. I had a great sense of freedom. This experience made exorcism real for me. It helped me understand why those who have not experienced exorcism may not appreciate its value in helping people discover, develop and heal their spiritual lives. We will come back to exorcism in Chapter 9 on page 133, on healing spiritual life.

Exorcism is perhaps the most dramatic evidence of the reality of spiritual evil and the importance of Jesus' victory on the Cross. My experience had validated what the Bible taught and made the supernatural dimension real to me. My spiritual eyes had been opened and I had discovered the very hidden reason why things go wrong in the world. At the time I thought (wrongly) that I had figured out all the reasons why things go wrong. But instead of my life getting better it was about to get worse. Much worse. As we have seen, life is a test of faith where we grow spiritually through suffering. My next lessons would be the trauma of a career loss that led me to the discovery of self-deception and a new identity as Father John. Following that I share an amazing discovery that came many years later as I was editing the manuscript. I discovered mental strongholds, as in the strong man of the Bible. This comes after the next chapter on self-deception because it is a very destructive combination of supernatural Satanic oppression and the natural mental process of self-deception.

Chapter 5

Discovering Self-Deception

Lucille and I married in 1979 with Christopher serving as "Best Boy" and our friends Geoff Machin as Best Man and Helen Meller as Bridesmaid. It was the opposite of most weddings — a $200.00 church service and a $100.00 reception. As a licensed server, I served the common cup to the guests during the Communion part of the service. Lucille was invited to sit in the Bishop's Chair. This was an idyllic time as we bought a small house in Rosedale and began our family — David was born in 1983 and Mary 14 months later in 1984.

I was a leader in the library profession and served as President of the Library Association of Alberta. As President elect of the Library Association of Alberta, I had invited Yoneji Masuda to come from Japan and speak at our annual Jasper Conference. He was considered the leading world authority on computerization and had just published *The New Information Society*. This conference motivated the Alberta Government, academic and public libraries, to work together in developing policies, procedures and a computer network to share access to library collections. This is now called The Alberta Library. When the position of Library Director came up in Red Deer Alberta in 1983 this seemed like a logical next move.

During the interview, the Red Deer Public Library Board seemed very interested in library automation as a way of improving library service in the city and region. It seemed like the perfect opportunity at a time when I had just been passed over for a promotion. It was very bad timing for the family. Lucille was having a second difficult pregnancy. She had been on bed rest for 3 months during her first pregnancy and needed the support of the high-risk pregnancy doctors in Calgary. I was very unwise in not leaving her in Calgary when we moved to Red Deer to begin my new job as Director of the Public Library in January. It was tremendously exciting. I bought my first personal computer in 1984. It was a Kaypro 10 with a stunning 10 megabytes of memory. At the Red Deer Public Library I began working on the library automation project. Our Technical Services Librarian was one of the few librarians in Canada with the technical expertise necessary to define computer specifications, solicit bids and evaluate proposals. At the same time I was also working on some of the other priorities of the board. For example there were no real job descriptions. I developed standard job descriptions and a new salary scale; to ensure more fairness based on the education, experience and training required. The Board established a community sub-committee to survey library needs and priorities.

The Board also wanted me to work with the Regional Public Library System, and include them in our automation plans. This was doomed from the start. Their headquarters was a nearby next town and their Director was coasting into retirement. The Director and Board members were not interested in computers and fearful of losing control. They complained to my Board that I was not listening to them and moving too fast. Instead of pausing and encouraging my Board to do their political work with the Regional Library Board first, I pushed on before everyone was onside.

I was politically naive and going too fast and in too many directions. It was also very stressful at home in June 1984. Mary had been born 10 weeks premature. I was there and facing the birth evaluation chart on the wall. The scale on the chart had "dark color," "not moving," "trouble breathing" as signs the baby was in serious trouble. She was put on 98% oxygen (the maximum) and moved to Intensive Care. During the third night, three doctors came into our room at different times and told us "Mary is very sick." They were preparing us for the worst. One lung was the size of a peanut shell and the other undeveloped. She did not come home for ten months and was on oxygen for two years. This experience traumatized me but also taught me to love unconditionally, pray for healing and depend on God as explained in Chapter 9 on page 133.

After the first year, the Red Deer Public Library Board members were having trouble with my "take charge" approach. They had become used to doing much of the library management themselves — including signing cheques. I thought I was listening, keeping them well informed and working very hard to do a good job. Unfortunately, my understanding of my role as the professional Library Director (to direct operations), was not shared. They were used to a more politically aware and passive Library Director, who took better direction on the details from the Board.

To make a long story short they suddenly decided to conduct a performance review as I was (news to me), apparently still on probation after 18 months. A very long and open ended questionnaire was circulated among the Board, Staff and selected community members. This revealed (big surprise) that I had offended some people with my "high handed" approach to management, including political relations with the Regional Library Director and his Board. They were afraid of losing their town's comfortable place as the centre of the regional library system.

Eighteen months after my appointment, there was a special Board Meeting late on Friday afternoon before a long weekend. Three Board members were away. I was given a letter, advising me that my performance was unsatisfactory and my ("probationary"?) position as Library Director was terminated effective immediately. I was completely stunned. It was like a road to Damascus experience. Like the Apostle Paul on the way to arrest Christians in Damascus, it felt like I had been knocked off my horse by a blinding light, and was sitting on the ground, with my assumption of being a very successful Library Director shattered. I did not know what to do or say. I drove home, told my wife and children the news and sat vacantly in the back yard for hours. My priest visited and offered help. I could have a small office in the Church to get away from the noise of Mary's oxygen concentrator and think. A lawyer friend was contacted and legal proceedings began. I began considering and applying for other opportunities.

My mind was completely boggled by the question of how could someone with such a good mind and so much education and experience, not have seen this coming? This was a traumatic example of things going wrong. My understanding of reality of the situation was obviously very different from that of others. My assumption that the human mind processes information completely and logically must be wrong. There had been warning signs. People had taken me aside and gently suggested I go slowly until everyone was onside politically. Somehow the warnings had been neglected. I could not seem to remember or focus on them. They somehow got overruled by my pride and determination to overcome the natural human opposition to change.

Eventually, there was a blinding flash of insight — the somehow had a name. Its name was "self-deception." It was an epiphany moment. I had discovered that my rational thinking process was fallible. The whole edifice of my pride and reliance on human reason to understand what was going on crumbled. The discovery of both spiritual evil and self-deception destroyed my faith in human reason and the liberal intellectualism I had assumed would guide me in life.

While the long, slow process of finding another job and my legal case dragged on, it seemed important to do some reading and research on self-deception. This is what librarians do. They know that they can learn how to do almost anything by reading about it and talking to experts. My new computer and printer moved into the "upper room" at St. Luke's. I used my time between applying for jobs to read about self-deception and reflect on my lack of awareness of other people's feelings.

Since I am a writer by nature, this grew into a manuscript of over 150 pages, with the working title, *Seven Great Deceptions: A Survival*

Manual For Pilgrims. As the months went by, the original plan unfortunately became sidetracked into what my mentor described as "a philosophy of John." It was revised, sent to a publisher and rejected. By this time I had moved to Toronto, to study for ordained ministry, and the project was abandoned. The discovery of how our minds naturally deceive us has helped me to understand myself and been a key learning in preparing me for twenty-five years of healing ministry and developing a deeper spiritual life.

I discovered that the Philosopher Herbert Fingarette[11] had suggested three possible ways for us to logically "engage" with new information that threatens our existing assumptions of truth and reality:

- Forego or abandon the "engagement" — reject the information
- Avow it as our own and accept responsibility — deal with it
- "Engage" ourselves but refuse to acknowledge the engagement as ours — to both know and not know the new information

This was a very helpful way of describing the problem of self-deception as both knowing and not-knowing new information that contradicts an existing assumption of truth. This explains, for example, why people who are emotionally attached to a religious or political viewpoint may not really hear arguments that contradict their convictions. This was the final answer I discovered to the question of why things go wrong. It should warn us of the vital importance of understanding how self-deception can work to "make things go wrong" — like my brief career as a Library Director.

Psychology teaches us that our minds can suppress, distort and hide vital information from us. This was a stunning discovery for me. It was based on reading the historic psychological work of Freud, Jung and Goleman.

Freud had begun helping people who were considered mentally weak. They were often suicidal, hysterical, spoke gibberish or were dysfunctional due to depression. They were an embarrassment to families, and sent to asylums where they could be cared for until they either recovered or died. Freud developed what he called the "Talking Therapy." He listened until he could decipher the mumbling and gibberish into words and sentences. At first these patients, mostly women, could not remember what had happened. By persisting in questioning and listening, Freud was able to gradually help them recall the traumatic event or situation that had caused their condition. The traumatic memory had apparently been blotted out of their conscious memory. As they were gradually able to recall and talk about the traumatic memory, their minds gradually healed.

Freud, the devout Jew, was doing the same work as a Christian priest. He was hearing a confession, assuring recovery, and releasing people from the emotional or spiritual bondage to the trauma. He was acting as a "soul doctor." "Freud changed the whole concept of mental illness by showing it was not the result of a weakness of intellect or a malfunction of the brain, but the impact of intense emotions on mental functioning."[12]

> "He reached another revolutionary conclusion, that the blocking out of an unpleasant idea from consciousness is an essential cause of hysteria, or what we later called neurosis."[13]

Freud's most basic discovery was the existence of the subconscious as a separate part of the mind. Not only was there an unconscious part, but the unconscious part was much bigger and more powerful than the conscious part.[14] His key discovery was that the unconscious part of the mind is very vulnerable to deception. Powerful emotions seem to be able to override our normal logical thinking. "Finally he realized that the *unconscious part of the mind lacked a sense of reality* (emphasis mine). It *did not distinguish between truth and emotionally charged fiction*. That was the greatest secret."[15]

This is how I had deceived myself. I was emotionally committed to computerization and had blotted out and over-ridden the logic of local politics. I discovered that the mind itself could be a deceiver! This is why you cannot talk to a terrorist and convert them to liberal democracy.

Freud defined three ways in which the human mind could work against the general secular assumption of the open, logical and complete processing of information — Repression, Resistance and Transference.

Repression can be defined as "a process by which unacceptable desires or impulses are excluded from consciousness and left to operate in the unconscious."[16] Many of Freud's patients had had horrendous sexual abuse. It was so traumatic that their minds could not handle it, and had pushed it down into the unconscious part of their mind. This working of the mind to both know, and to not know, had overloaded the mind and led to a collapse.

Resistance is a term used by Freud to explain a patient's difficulty in recalling an unpleasant or unwanted event. Psychology students are sometimes shown a short video of a basketball game to help them understand resistance. In the middle of a very active basketball game, a woman wearing a white dress and carrying a white umbrella, walks across the middle of the action on the court for eight seconds. After watching the video, students are asked questions about the video. None of them ever remembers seeing the woman. Their minds have automatically filtered her out, as unwanted noise or a distraction. This is another way in which our minds can deceive us.

Transference is a fairly common tendency of counselling clients to see the analyst or counsellor as some personage from their childhood; a mother, father etc., and transfer inappropriate feelings to them. Women, for example, may think they are in love with their priest or counsellor. Transference can also refer to the patient who confuses illusion with reality. "Transference is probably one of the most common reasons for human error and conflict, in sizing up reality. It makes us see the world through the glasses of our own wishes and fears, and consequently makes us confuse illusion with reality."[17]

Freud had helped me understand why things go wrong as a result of normal mental processes that are designed to protect the mind from exposure to information that has emotional baggage. This can lead to self-deception through incomplete or incorrect information. His work was much misunderstood at the time because of his stormy relationships with his colleagues (a gunfighter perhaps). There were also very serious mistranslations of his work. For example "die Seele" (the Soul) was consistently mistranslated as "mental processes" in an apparent attempt to make the new discipline of Psychology sound less religious and more scientific for consumption in North America."[18]

Daniel Goleman, the bestselling author on emotional Intelligence wrote *Vital Lies, Simple Truths: The Psychology of Self-Deception* in 1985. It was for me the right book at the right time. Goleman worked with patients "… whose very disorders seemed to protect them from some deeper threat."[19] This was similar to Freud who discovered that repressing memories of traumatic events, often sexual abuse, had overloaded their minds and made them dysfunctional. Goleman also realized that self-deception is a by-product of a mental process, that protects us from emotionally threatening or traumatic information. What actually comes to our conscious mind "… is a delicate balance between vigilance inattention."[20] This is how he explained our ability to both know but not know at the same time.

Self-Deception is the result of a natural process. Our brains could be overloaded by all of the detailed information collected by our senses. For example our heartbeat and breathing are normally controlled out of awareness. Only when we are frightened or exercising do we tend to notice what is going on in our body. This information is normally filtered out before reaching our conscious attention or awareness.

Goldman developed a synthesis of Neurology and Psychology, to explain the difference between the logical and the emotional parts of the human brain. Our brains apparently have two separate paths for information that developed as the primitive human brain evolved from dealing with simple fight or flight survival reactions (the emotions), to the much later logical part, which can do a much more complex analysis of situations. His point is that we need both. The emotional information adds (spiritual) values and preferences to enrich the logical analysis, so we make better decisions.

The take-away for me was the discovery that self-deception, as a natural human mental process, was a another reason why things go wrong. This discovery demolished my intellectualism and faith in the human mind and reason as a completely reliable way of discovering truth. It also taught me to be very careful in trying to understand how things work in the supernatural dimension. Self-deception is one of the key lessons in life that I would like to share with my children and others to save them a lot of grief and pain.

Chapter 6

Discovering Mental Strongholds

> "An individual mental stronghold is a way of thinking and feeling that has developed a life of its own within us."[21]

Strongholds are the mental prisons that Jesus came to free people from by proclaiming the Good News to the poor, opening the eyes of the blind and *freeing the captives*. (Luke 4.18) Strongholds are at the heart of the teaching and healing ministry of Jesus and our mission as Christians. Jesus ministry was to both teach and heal people.

This discovery is the hinge of the book. In the previous chapters on spiritual evil and self-deception we saw how first demonic influences and then natural psychological processes can independently lead to self-deception and things going wrong in our lives. In this chapter we will see how these two can work together to build a destructive mental stronghold in our minds that blinds us to truth and reality. Mental strongholds are a combination of demonic influence and the natural process of self-deception working together to blind people to truth and develop spiritually destructive patterns of belief. Satan tempts us build strongholds in our soul out of our natural human weaknesses, desires fears and the natural self-deception process. The mental strongholds of intellectualism and liberalism are what I have had to overcome to fully discover, develop and heal my life.

In the final stages of editing the manuscript I was blessed by a visit to my long-time mentor John Sandford and his son Mark in Coeur d'Alene Idaho. It was an awesome privilege, and humbling experience of love, to have this great pioneer in the healing ministry go meticulously through my poor punctuation and questionable theology.

At our last meeting I asked him about strongholds. I needed to confirm what for me was an epiphany moment. I had just read his book *Deliverance and Inner Healing*, and discovered the chapter on individual and corporate strongholds.[22] Sandford had reminded me that God created us in His own image, and had to give us free will in order to have a genuine relationship of love. The danger in this is that we had to be free to reject God's offer of relationship and rebel against His authority. Satan, the archangel who was cast out of heaven for rebellion, is constantly deceiving and tempting men and women to join him in this rebellion. Satan supernaturally deceives and blinds human thinking to build destructive mental strongholds. Strongholds have a powerful life of their own in trying to control human souls. This is the opposite of God who gives us freedom.

The question I asked was "Are strongholds similar to what Jung called 'archetypes'?" I had never really understood Jung's explanation of archetypes. What Jung called the "collective unconsciousness" and the way it organized itself into clusters of ideas by emotional power, sounded very similar to Sandfords' much clearer definition of strongholds as a way of thinking and feeling that develops a life of its own. (The librarian in me is always interested how information is organized and retrieved.) Sandford said yes, and in an epiphany moment I realized that strongholds were the hidden something I had been trying to discover and name as the hidden reason why things go wrong.[23] My follow-up question was, "Are strongholds a form of spiritual bondage?" Another "yes" that led to a revision of the model for healing prayer ministry in Chapter 9 on page 133.

It was like finding the missing pieces in the centre of a puzzle that holds all the other pieces together. I realized that I had been wounded by my emotional abandonment as a child and mentally blinded by the strongholds of intellectualism and extreme liberalism. This had prevented me from discovering a spiritual life by listening to my heart (intuition), having the emotional intelligence necessary for successful relationships in my marriage and political success as a library director. This was the final answer to my question of "Why things go wrong." The *why* finally had an explanation and a name!

This discovery helped me understand how the mental strongholds of intellectualism, liberalism and homosexuality had combined to deceive church leaders into seeing nothing biblically wrong with same-sex blessings and marriage. The best example was a chance meeting with a retired bishop who told me the Canadian House of Bishops had given a delegation of men who had been healed of homosexuality a standing ovation for their courage in speaking out — but remained blinded to the obvious conclusion that if homosexuality can be healed by prayer, we should be offering prayer ministry and support for abstinence — not blessing a spiritually destructive mental stronghold.

> "It is true that we live in the world, but we do not fight from worldly motives. The weapons we use in our fight are not the world's weapons but God's powerful weapons, which we use to destroy strongholds. We destroy false arguments, we pull down every proud obstacle that is raised against the knowledge of God, we take every thought captive and make it obey Christ."
> (2 Corinthians 10. 3-5)[24]

Sandfords' book *Deliverance and Inner Healing* helped me understand this passage and how I had become blinded by strongholds. The Holy Spirit finally opened my eyes so I could see the blindingly obvious truth of this teaching, and apply it to my own life.

The sword of the Holy Spirit is the spirit of truth. Lucille and I pray for this sword to help us see and beat back the lies of the enemy every morning.

"The foremost activity of Satan is to capture the minds of men and women and thus their souls. The mind is the citadel of the soul."[25] Is that the same book? Here Sandford is giving us the big picture. He is opening our spiritual eyes to warn us of the danger our spiritual lives face every day. This helped me understand why people trapped in the mental strongholds of intellectualism, extreme liberalism, homosexuality, racism and religious fundamentalism are so hard to talk to. Their self-deception and strongholds have blinded then to contrary information.

I had obviously picked up my intellectual and liberalism patterns of thinking and feeling in childhood. In our family you were rewarded emotionally only for knowing what was going on internationally and politically. I had to demonstrate knowledge and cleverness to be part of the conversation. The lack of warm affection and emotional support, led naturally to feelings of insecurity, fear and performance orientation. Fear, insecurity and selfishness are the main weapons of Satan in tempting us into sin. He tries to keep us self-focused so we do not hear the voice of the Holy Spirit.

Emotional deprivation led to having a "slumbering spirit" that was not picking up intuitive or emotional information. My low emotional intelligence let to a failed marriage relationship and professional disaster. Satan had used my natural self-deceptions process to build strongholds. I had not really heard or understood key Biblical teachings on the forgiveness of sin and the guidance of the Holy Spirit. "The function of an individual mental stronghold is to keep the person from thinking effectively, or feeling repentant or praying in ways that would defeat it as one of the fortresses of the ruling centre of flesh within the person."[26] My strongholds of intellectualism and liberalism were growing stronger as I did not really know about the danger of sin, spiritual oppression and the freedom of repentance and confession.

Strongholds become the landing places for demons which can

then be more effective in oppressing people from the inside. Jesus refers to the more powerful demons as the "Strongman" who must be bound before he can be cast out. "In fact, no one can enter a strong man's house without first tying him up. Then he can plunder the strong man's house." (Mark 3.27) Jesus is not talking about worldly crime here. In the surrounding verses He is talking about Satan not being divided and the forgiveness of sin.

In prayer ministry for the destruction of a personal stronghold, The Sandfords often began with silent prayer to bind the strongman before they could guide the counselee. When the strongman is spiritually bound, the person is better able to see how they have built up a mental stronghold by believing lies and rebelling against God. Then it is easier to plunder and remove the demons and the sin-guilt they are feeding on. In chapter 9 on healing we will see how personal strongholds and bondages can be dismantled and broken through prayer ministry including the repentance, confession and absolution of sin.

Other common patterns of thinking and feeling Sandford mentions as strongholds include racism, homosexuality, sexual sin, abortion, humanism and "carnal theology" — which I refer to (more generally) as extreme liberal theology. As we will see in the healing chapter below, these mental structures grow stronger in us through experiences of emotional trauma and sin. These experiences separate us from our conscience and the guidance of the Holy Spirit. The primary function of strongholds is to confuse and blind people so they do not really hear sermons, advice and the voice of reason which may be contrary to the way of thinking or feeling of the stronghold. This is why you cannot negotiate rationally with a religious terrorist.

The love of Lucille woke up my slumbering spirit and freed me from the emotional blinding of my strongholds. My experience confirms what Isaiah, Jesus and John Sandford all say about how to set people free from strongholds:

1. Proclaim the Good News, (Luke 4.18) — the truth to the lie

2. Persistent applications of love and truth[27]

This discovery has helped me adopt a more loving and pastoral attitude in the current debate in the Anglican Church of Canada over same-sex blessing and marriage. My own stronghold of intellectualism and ignorance of strongholds have sidetracked me into destructive feelings of anger at extreme liberal clergy for over 25 years. Now I understand that they too are unwitting victims of the powerful combination of natural and supernatural deception called strongholds in the Bible. This discovery has profound implications for how the church should relate to the gay and lesbian community. Instead of condemnation or phoney blessings and marriage, we should be treating them like everyone else and offering the good news of forgiveness-in-Jesus, freedom from strongholds and emotional support.

6.1 Corporate Strongholds

"A corporate stronghold is a way of thinking, feeling and acting that is built into the common mentality we all share."[28] Sandford uses the example of what happened in Germany as the strongholds of racism, war and aggression rapidly poisoned the culture under Nazi leadership. Hitler tapped into the basic fears of the German people following their humiliation in WW 1. He offered the lie of Jewish responsibility as a scapegoat for the insecurities, fears and latent racism of the German people. He gave people hope that their national pride could be restored after the defeat in WW1. The twin strongmen or strongholds of racism and war /aggression, became the driving force of the nation and led to the evil destruction of the Holocaust.

The good news is that Sandford also shared with me that he had led a workshop on healing strongholds for German pastors. One pastor had taken this teaching to East Berlin, and started building a new national foundation of mass personal repentance, confession and prayer for forgiveness. This is what broke the power of the strongman and led to the dramatic fall of the Berlin Wall as described above.

My epiphany moment in Coeur d'Alene went beyond discovering the bondage of personal strongholds. I have been in a state of trauma and grief over the state of the Anglican Church ever since I discovered the authenticity of the supernatural Biblical worldview in the 1980s. I have watched in horror as a majority of the Anglican Church of Canada slid deeper and deeper into a new liberal theology which de-emphasized the supernatural worldview of the Bible, the healing miracles of Jesus and the evil influence of Satan as mythical exaggerations My epiphany moment included being able to understand this as a corporate stronghold and understand why so many of the leaders in the Church are impervious to reason and the evidence of homosexual men and lesbian women being freed from this stronghold through prayer ministry in Canada and the US.

Sandford reserves his harshest criticism for the extreme evangelical churches in the US that have fallen into the corporate stronghold of what he calls "carnal theology."[29] As you will see below we have both been deeply troubled by what I call the extreme liberal deconstruction of the Bible. Sandford focuses on a new conservative evangelical theology. He calls it a "half-gospel" developed by evangelical pastors to simplify Christianity for a more mobile postwar generation. First they reduced the Gospel to a one-time conversion experience of salvation. This meant cutting out the lifelong follow-up work of sanctification (becoming holy/*Going Spiritual*). Then they made an idol out of being saved. The problem is that many of these saved people do not know or believe that they could still fall into sin and become demonized. This prideful attitude allowed them to develop a stronghold of carnal (worldly) evangelical theology with no need to repent and confess sins. This sadly cut them off from seeking and receiving the healing and forgiveness they needed.[30]

In Canada we have seen the devastating effects of this narrow corporate stronghold of extreme evangelical theology or evangelicalism. "Isms" are, by definition, corporate strongholds. Many of our clergy have been tempted by the simple and easy path of teaching this half-gospel of salvation, without the harder work of guiding people towards sanctification (*Going Spiritual*) — the lifelong work of discovering, developing and healing spiritual life. This approach is particularly attractive to less educated preachers and TV evangelists. They promise salvation without any ongoing need for serious self-examination, repentance and confession. This is like a vaccination against catching serious Christianity. People believe they are saved and all they have to do is be good, attend church and give money. They have a religion without a real spiritual life.

It gets worse. Many of these people eventually realized they were starving for something more. They kept reading about love in the Bible and then seeing less than loving judgementalism in their church. Many ran to churches which were less evangelical and more loving and liberal in theology. Unfortunately many ran right to the end of the spectrum of extreme liberal theology. Some of these are now our bishops and leading the campaign to re-interpret the Bible. They have revised the historic Christian teachings on sin and redemptions to accommodate the political demands the gay and lesbian community.

Protestant churches in North America are now deeply divided and polarized as a result of this demonically inspired stronghold. I explain this as a spectrum between the extreme poles of law without love (evangelical) and love without law (liberal):

Figure 6.1

This is of course illogical as law is essentially how love is defined and love is what drives and leads to law. Anything less than a church in perfect balance between law and love is by definition dysfunctional. These churches are not going to help people discover, develop and heal their spiritual lives as we will see in Chapter 8 on page 113.

Sandford's warning on the stronghold of carnal (worldly) evangelical theology should be nailed to the door of every evangelical church:

> "I firmly believe that Satan's master plan was first to destroy the natural family and then the church. Through the false doctrine of total instant change he planned to bring down the Church and disgrace it before the world. Through liberalism, modernism, humanism and the strongholds of homosexuality and abortion he has shorn most main line denominations of their effectiveness for Christ. Many churches and entire denominations now champion the very cases the Lord hates, unaware that they are being used as pawns by corporate strongholds controlled by spiritual forces of darkness in the heavenly places."

As I have painfully discovered challenging a corporate stronghold alone is a futile and self-destructive mission. Sandford proposes six steps in healing a corporate stronghold.[31]

1. We must come to see clearly how they hook into people's flesh, so that repentance can remove the barbs of Satan's attacks.

2. We must repent our own sin and responsibility for the stronghold so we can see clearly.

3. We must get clear guidance from God the Holy Spirit and *not act without God's command to act*. Getting ahead of God will lead to more, not less, demonic oppression.

4. We must learn to fight as an army. "We should understand that our foremost weapon is ...repentance on behalf of those trapped by the principality."[32] Sandford warns churches not to rebuke strongholds or principalities without clear corporate guidance and serious corporate repentance.

5. Be prepared for counterattack. While we have the victory in Jesus, there is always serious blowback after spiritual warfare.

6. Persevere. "Encounters with corporate strongholds and principalities are not solitary battles: they are long-term conflicts."

This teaching has eased the burden and grief in my life over what had happened in the past and freed me for a more joyful and powerful ministry of teaching and healing prayer in the future. Now we go back over 30 years to the story of how I discovered my new identity as a priest and learned how to develop and heal my spiritual life.

Chapter 7

Discovering Father John

Father John is both a fun and a serious way of describing the amazing new identity that was gradually emerging. I was struggling through the sudden loss of my identity as a successful library director, the challenges of finding a new professional job and caring for a baby on oxygen and clinging to life. Father John is a bit of a caricature and more fun than Rev. Gishler. It is fun because I would like to see myself grow into a kindly old priest, who has brought freedom, healing and joy to others. The title father is also a serious spiritual distinction. It suggests a more mystical, sacramental, or Roman Catholic/Orthodox description of the role of a priest, in fathering a spiritual life in others. The alternatives of "Reverend" and "Pastor," in my mind, suggest the more formal religious authority and pastoral care roles of a priest.

The first serious suggestion of my new identity came during a conversation with John Dutton, then Director of the Calgary Public Library. I was having trouble getting a new professional library job — in spite of having just been President of the Library Association of Alberta, and planning the largest annual conference in its history. John was very kind to me, and, as I was leaving, said quietly, "Have you ever thought of doing a 180?" I was stunned. What did he mean I asked? He was suggesting I consider ordained ministry. There probably had been other hints, like the voice in my head thinking I could preach a better sermon during church services; but this was the one that really got my attention.

Going all the way back to high school in Edmonton in the early 1960s I could remember organizing and leading a very moving worship service as president of the AYPA, the (sadly now defunct) Anglican Young Peoples Association. There was a sense of the holy, community and the mystical as we had lit some candles and prayed together.

My favourite mentor was the Rev. Canon Herbie O'Driscoll, who taught wonderful courses at the Sorrento Centre near Salmon Arm in B.C. He was so popular that the same group of "Herbie" fans gathered each summer for a week of teaching and recreation. Herbie was a story teller in the best Irish tradition. The text of the story was almost irrelevant, compared to the profound insights he added. He could probably spin *The Three Little Pigs* out for an hour. Herbie made the Biblical message come to life. These were real people with real issues and fears. One afternoon he had us do a Bible skit outside on the lawn. There I was in my bathrobe costume playing Jesus talking to the Samaritan woman. I came to the words:

> Jesus answered her, "If you knew the gift of God and who it is that asks you for a drink, you would have asked him and he would have given you living water." .... "Sir," the woman said, "I can see that you are a prophet. Our ancestors worshiped on this mountain, but you Jews claim that the place where we must worship is in Jerusalem." "Woman," Jesus replied, "believe me, a time is coming when you will worship the Father neither on this mountain nor in Jerusalem. You Samaritans worship what you do not know; we worship what we do know, for salvation is from the Jews. Yet a time is coming and has now come when the true worshipers will worship the Father in the Spirit and in truth, for they are the kind of worshipers the Father seeks. God is spirit, and his worshipers must worship in the Spirit and in truth." The woman said, "I know that Messiah"

(called Christ) "is coming. When he comes, he will explain everything to us." Then Jesus declared, "I, the one speaking to you, am he." (John 4, 10;19-26 NIV)

There was a very, very long silence as the power of what I had just said washed over me. This was a profound moment of emotion as the truth of what I had just said hung in the air. I knew in my heart that Jesus really did exist and that it was possible to know him personally. This is one of my first steps in developing a spiritual life. I went from knowing about Jesus to knowing Jesus personally, from admiring Jesus to being in love with Him. Much later at a Healing Workshop the leader asked us all to share when Jesus became a real person for them as an ice breaker. This was my story.

Herbie later led a preaching workshop in Manitoba and gave the best advice I have ever received on preaching. I used his "twenty questions to ask about a sermon" to train and evaluate lay readers when I was in Holland-Glenboro Parish. His most profound warning was to tell us that every time we preached there would be at least one desperate person listening: someone who had just lost a job, a marriage, a friend or relative to death or found they had an incurable disease. His voice rose as he warned — "do not let that person leave the church without hope!"

Another mentor was William Barclay, whose famous commentaries on the books of the New Testament, *The Daily Study Bible*, are still in print. I purchased all 16 volumes and used them for leading Bible study groups, daily devotions and sermon preparation. At seminary I found there was often more useful information on a passage in them, than in all the other commentaries combined. Barclay divides a Book of the Bible into short segments followed by a half page commentary that is both scholarly and practical. Almost everyone I know who has developed a serious spiritual life has gone through the experience of first reading the whole Bible, then studying the Bible story and eventually knowing and becoming part of the Bible story of God reaching out to individuals.

Dreams are a Biblical way of spiritual discernment. Jung pioneered in discovering that we all have a huge volume of information stored in our sub-conscious or unconscious mind. The filters that protect our conscious mind from being overwhelmed with detail and anxiety-causing information seem to weaken during sleep. This allows fragments of information into our conscious but sleeping mind through dreams. Often this information is coded in symbolic form. For example a railroad track has two tracks which never meet. A dream involving a railroad track can be a warning of conflict. Two is the number of conflict.

I was fortunate in finding a Jungian analyst in Calgary who helped me decipher my dreams over eight years. One dream that recurred several time involved me wandering around a school or university looking for the classroom I was supposed to be in. These were very distressing as I could not remember my timetable or find my place. That was of course the message. I was searching for my place, my identity.

A trip to Israel also led to the discovery of my identity as Father John. Lucille and I wanted to have children before she reached high-risk age. We also wanted to see all the places we had been reading about in the Bible. It was not a convenient time, as I was in the middle of planning a Provincial Library Conference and we had invited Yoneji Masuda, author of *The New Information Society* to come from Japan as our speaker. But the trip to Israel was urgent for us, as we might not get another opportunity to travel until our children were grown, and mostly because God had a plan for us.

Changing flights in Frankfurt shocked us into the reality of Palestinian terrorism. It was not long after a massacre of Israeli Olympic athletes at the airport and security was very serious. Lucille was shocked when two female guards took her aside for a strip search. Later as we were loaded onto a special bus and driven to the Israeli jet at the far end of the runway, I noticed sharpshooters on the roof of the building and armed soldiers under each wing. Looking around at the dozen other young men, I noticed that they all had the same dark curly beard and Jewish nose as me. I turned to Lucille and said "Moshe, we are going home!" That was the feeling we had at all the places we visited: Jerusalem, Bethlehem, Nazareth,

Capernaum, the Dead Sea and Masada.

We met some Christian Palestinians on our first day in Jerusalem and talked all day and into the night. We ended up walking through the darkened streets of the Old City of Jerusalem, with a dead chicken for an evening meal at a friends restaurant. We left Israel with a much deeper understanding of the conflict. We also met a reporter who told us how Israel controls all news leaving the country.

Israel is also a spiritually dangerous place. Spiritual people (as opposed to religious or political people) can often feel the tension in the air around them. The spiritual battle is so intense, that more than one American pastor has had the traumatic experience of coming to Israel, and completely losing his faith. For us it was the opposite. As we stood on the mountaintop fortress of Masada, where the Jewish rebels made their last stand and 900 had committed suicide rather than be captured and enslaved by Rome, we knew our destiny. For Israel there is no surrender and no cost too great. Like Isaiah setting his face like flint, I realized Christian Faith is by definition a serious fight to the death. I do not wear a cross for decoration but as a reminder of the cost of my salvation.

My new identity came to me at the Wailing Wall in Jerusalem. The Wailing Wall is all that is left of the foundation of the Second Temple. Jerusalem was completely destroyed by the Romans in AD 75. The specific order for destruction was so that a plow could be drawn across the city. The remaining retaining wall for the Temple foundation is built of huge squared stones one metre by one metre by ten metres long. Many people put small pieces of paper with prayers in the cracks between the stones. I simply raised my hands in silent prayer with my fingers gently touching the stones. I felt a great sense of peace and blessing as someone called to serve in ministry as a priest.

Another discernment moment came later during a three day Cursillo weekend. "Cursillo" is a Spanish word that means "short course." The Cursillo weekend is similar to the Alpha Course with lots of singing and fifteen talks followed by table group discussions.

The goal of the weekend is to help people focus on discovering and experiencing their spiritual life in an authentic Christian community of love. This is preparation for continuing fellowship and encouragement through regular bi-weekly grouping with men or women.

The whole weekend is supported around the clock by prayer. The constant sense of being loved and the experience of forgiveness and deep healing are transformative. What broke me was the letter from the lady in Japan who was praying for John Gishler in Calgary all weekend. If you haven't "got it" about the love of Jesus, you will. Cursillo and the similar Alpha Course (completed by over 18 million people worldwide), are revitalizing Christianity. Many people would join me in saying "It changed my life." Go for it when you get the chance!

My lay ministry in Red Deer grew from purely social visits in hospital to include brief prayers for healing. As we will come to in Chapter 9 on page 133, we still had a very sick little girl at home. Mary was on oxygen for two years. Her birth had brought us to our knees in prayer, and taught us to pray for healing. My lay ministry was expanding to services outside of Red Deer for other clergy during vacations. I had very positive feedback on my teaching. They still remember my "Star Wars" explanations of evil and the Holy Spirit. My favourite story is about my son David, who at 5 was trying to figure out why Darth Vader (the bad guy in Star Wars movies) was always so angry and destructive. He interrupted my confused answer with his bright blue eyes shining saying "you mean he doesn't know about Jesus." And a little child shall lead them....

Three more experiences confirmed my new identity as Father John. The first was when Lucille was driving me between a lay led worship service in Lacombe and another in Rimbey. The assigned Bible readings I was preaching on included Isaiah 50.7:

> "Because the Sovereign Lord helps me, I will not be disgraced. Therefore have I **set** my **face like flint**, and I know I will not be put to shame."

As I was reviewing my teaching notes, these words jumped off the page at me. I had a very powerful sense that this is what I had to choose to do to be an effective and authentic teacher. This decision has cost me and my family a lot. The church is a very political environment. I was, and still am considered too conservative and too evangelical by many more liberal clergy. It has been a long, hard, and losing battle. Our Church has had twenty years of continuous "dialogues" on homosexual clergy, women priests and gay marriage. These went on and on for years until those like me, who had set their face like flint and dissented, were outvoted.

Another key discovery experience was during an Evening Prayer service at Sylvan Lake. I had borrowed a priest's robe and at the end gave the blessing. I said "May the grace of our Lord Jesus Christ and the love of God and the fellowship of the holy Spirit be with you all, this day, and forevermore." As I drew a huge cross in the air, I had a profound sense that this was not John Gishler the librarian dressed up as a priest. This was John Gishler the priest — dressed the way he was supposed to be dressed. It was like a divine yes.

It was time to talk to my priest and my bishop. This led to a long process of screening by a Diocesan Committee and the National Advisory Committee on Postulants For Ordination. The latter consisted of a psychologist, priest and layperson. They each had a file four inches thick on me, based on pages of questions to four people who knew me well. I waited nervously outside on the lawn with two other candidates. It was stressful as the Committee members are required to read the whole file, interview, pray and then say either yes or no. They said yes to all three of us and our lives changed forever.

The last big hurdle of course was provision. We had two children just starting school. We would have to move and live somewhere for three years while I studied for a Master of Divinity Degree. We had visited Wycliffe College in Toronto on our way home from Israel and decided this would give me the best education. The other universities were closer to the grandparents, but seemed either too theologically liberal or too second rate. My father generously offered to help, but finances were still weighing on my mind when we were at the tea after my father-in-law's funeral in Calgary. It was across a tea table that Rachel Meller, mother of Lucille's best friend Helen and a former missionary in China said: "John, why would you want to serve the God of the whole universe, if he could not find a few thousand dollars to get you through university?" Looking into the eyes of this wonderful servant of God, I felt both ashamed of my lack of faith and honoured to be in such company. There was no way back.

7.1 Wycliffe College:
The Battle for the Bible

There are seven seminaries associated with the University of Toronto. This was the best academic training available in Canada. But it was an academic degree and not always very spiritual. Most distressing for me was the required Bible 101 Course. This was an exposure to faculty from every college. Each professor taught their specialty. For someone who had just had his life changed after discovering the authenticity of the Biblical supernatural worldview, the lectures felt like a shredding of the Bible. I learned about all the errors and inconsistencies in the text, how it included author and cultural bias, and was largely mythical and written long after the time of Jesus. Had I not set my face like flint, I could have lost my faith. This was a dramatic introduction to a new intellectual liberal theology that has since become normative. It's misguided intellectual deconstruction of the Bible text is destroying the mainline churches.

This liberal "progressive" deconstruction of biblical orthodoxy has been the thorn in my side since ordination in 1991. My most viewed blog post has been on the dramatic differences between orthodox Christianity and a new liberal theology — *Same-Sex Marriage and the Challenge of Liberal Theology*.

I have spent the last 25 years trying to teach a more balanced and authentic spiritual interpretation of the Bible in the midst of a fierce theological battle. On one side many academics and theological liberals regard the Bible as a largely mythical Jewish cultural document that is not necessarily divinely inspired. At the other extreme are evangelical fundamentalists who insist that every word was audibly spoken by God to spiritual men who copied it down without error.

Neither side is really listening to what the Bible is actually saying to them. As in political hardball, both sides are blinded by their opposing mental strongholds of liberalism and evangelicalism (see above). The focus is on crushing the other side. Neither side is really acknowledging the role of the Holy Spirit in guiding both the Biblical writers, and contemporary believers in interpreting the Bible. The consequence is that we now have two very different interpretations, two different religions and denominational splits in the Anglican and Lutheran churches of North America. For more information on this new liberal theology see http://www.spirituallifeteaching.info and Machen's *Christianity and Liberalism*.[33]

When I first read the Bible I was shocked and angry. I was shocked at the number of references to the Holy Spirit ("Spirit of God" in Genesis), healing miracles and the demonic. I was angry that I was not taught anything about the supernatural dimension in Sunday schools or sermons growing up. When I began experiencing the Holy Spirit, healing miracles and the demonic I felt betrayed by the church. How did these critical teachings get lost? What I discovered was that as the early church grew and spread out to avoid persecution, the leadership eventually made compromises with Roman governors for recognition and protection. Clergy training for the masses of new believers was delegated to academics. These academics did not necessarily have any personal experiences of the Holy Spirit, healing and the demonic. They would be particularly vulnerable to the mental stronghold of intellectualism (like me) and gradually become spiritually blinded to the reality of the supernatural dimension.

The orthodoxy of the Roman Catholic and Protestant churches has been seriously compromised by the hijacking of Christendom by intellectuals who did not always understand or appreciate the importance of the Holy Spirit as the continuing presence of Jesus in this world. Genuine prophecy and words of knowledge should have the same authority as the (continuing) text of the Bible. Human reason is not always a reliable authority in determining orthodoxy. The great church father Thomas Aquinas (1225-74) had skipped over Plato and gone further back to Aristotle's natural philosophy to develop his Church doctrines. These depended entirely on human sense perception and reason and denied the later Platonic third source of knowledge: "divine madness" or what Christians call the Holy Spirit.[34]

> "In the West, Augustine's habit of ascribing potency to internal grace rather than to the Holy Spirit, and the medieval substitution of the institutional church and its sacraments for the Spirit and the word, as bringing salvation, blocked serious pneumatology for centuries."[35]

The reality was, that the Church founded by Peter, was no longer to be guided by the Holy Spirit through spiritually anointed prophets, apostles and teachers, but by academics (like Aquinas) under the control of a pope. It was no different than the ancient Hebrew Sanhedrin; which also only paid lip service to divine guidance. This led to a low point in Western Christianity. The Protestant Reformation challenged the authority of the Roman Catholic Church over doctrinal orthodoxy, by insisting that the Bible was a higher authority than the Pope for orthodoxy.

During the Enlightenment academics, humanists and liberals began a process of questioning the authenticity of the Biblical texts — particularly the supernatural miracles and healings of Jesus. In our own time academics and liberal clergy have continued to deconstruct the supernatural worldview of the Bible, describing the miracles, resurrection of Jesus and accounts of supernatural evil as pre-scientific and mythical. Because they are blinded by the mental strongholds of intellectualism and liberalism they do not understand how the supernatural dimension operates. They cannot understand the holiness of God, the problem of sin separating people from God and the need for a divine Saviour who could provide a way to forgiveness and right relationship. This is all critical to the process of developing a personal spiritual life.

Wycliffe College required Divinity students to pass a course in biblical Greek. This was a huge challenge to me. I had failed Greek miserably in High School and was not gifted at languages. My most profound spiritual experience at Wycliffe was praying in the dark on a bench in Queens Park, and crying out to God. My Greek final was the next day. Without Greek I could not graduate or go on to ministry. As previously, when I fell in love with Lucille, I just cried out to God "Why did you have to bring me all the way here with a wife and children to slay me?" God answers prayer from the heart. I recognized and knew the Bible passage, and a wonderful Christian professor decided that 67% is close enough to 70% so I passed.

Greek was actually a very helpful part of my spiritual learning. The Greek language has more cases and declensions, which means it is more specific and precise than English. The Bible, for example, has many references to life "in Christ" and "in the Spirit." These phrases take on a more profound meaning when you know there is a dative case in Greek which specifically means physically inside. So these references are not mistranslations or obscure, but a very clear explanation of spiritual life. The Greek Bible is also much stronger in tone. For example our English Bibles typically read "and the Lord was angry." The original Greek is more like "God was extremely angry and about to destroy them."

My second student ministry placement was an incredible experience. I, who had grown up with highly educated and successful parents, surrounded by people with PhDs. reported to the Don Jail every Monday at 9:00 am, and was locked up with the inmates until lunchtime. My task was to simply be available. I would walk around the cell blocks and talk to anyone who wanted to talk. It opened up a whole new world to me. My mentor Father Mario was an incredible teacher who showed me everything: including the shaft where the gallows used to be, when the last two men were hanged in the old part of the jail. I had been aware of this as a teenager, and knew there was great doubt about their guilt at the time. It was amazing to talk to men who were drug dealers, thieves and rapists, and to share the good news of forgiveness through faith in Jesus.

I was also blessed by a double course on Spiritual Direction that proved enormously helpful in connecting people with the divine. The instructor was a Roman Catholic woman who connected me to the rich heritage of spiritual teachings and practices that the English Reformers had left behind when they broke away from the Roman Church. We learned spiritual direction by practicing in pairs for a whole academic year. We would sit in facing chairs, go to prayer and be affirming listeners, as the other person shared his weekly struggles with temptations and obstacles to spiritual life.

This proved helpful in my Clinical and Pastoral Education Course at Sick Children's Hospital in Toronto. I was put in a very challenging situation. My supervisor was about as theologically liberal as you can be. CPE is non-denominational pastoral counselling, based on the idea that simply being emotionally with and listening empathetically to people, as they go through a medical crisis, will give them comfort. It was very good for me, as I needed to learn how to relate to people emotionally. The down side was my supervisor did not believe in the power of the Holy Spirit and prayer. He even suggested I was being arrogant if I thought my prayers would make God do something differently. He was not just testing me. He insisted I place a doll on a bed, cover it with a sheet, and demonstrate for the class exactly what I would do and say. Fortunately I had had lots of experience with my daughter Mary, so we all learned something that day.

I have since learned that this non-biblical idea of an impassive God, and the denial of the supernatural worldview of the Bible, developed in the Church in response to fierce debates over Gnosticism. The supernatural role of the Holy Spirit was downplayed in the teachings of Thomas Aquinas who went back to Aristotle's philosophical idolatry of reason. This was developed by the Scholastics and Enlightenment philosophers into the modern stronghold of liberalism and non-biblical liberal theology. This liberal theology has replaced Plato's triad of reason, tradition and divine madness (Holy Spirit) as reliable sources of truth, with the self-deception/stronghold prone duo of reason and tradition. This explains why many modern clergy are not really interested in praying for healing.

My final test came a few weeks later. I was called to care for a young girl in intensive care. Pastoral Care in a hospital involves the emotional and spiritual needs of staff, patients and family members. Doctors encourage this pastoral help with families, as it frees them to focus on the medical issues. Cheryl had been in a van driven by her mother that was "T-boned" at high speed at a highway intersection. The other driver failed to notice a stop sign. As I met the mother on the hospital steps, I knew she would be somebody I could work with. She was carrying a large, well worn Bible. When the doctors had finished their work we were allowed into the operating room to pray for the Cheryl. Her brain was swelling so they put a drain in her skull to relieve the pressure. This went on for three days as the mother and I held Cheryl's hand, and covered her with prayers for healing and strength. Our prayers were answered. Cheryl went home after a few weeks of supervised rest and healing.

It was now time to graduate from Wycliffe and be ordained as a Deacon in the church of God. This is the last step before becoming a priest. Deacons in the ancient (and modern) church are the servants of the church. The Apostles ordained Stephen as a Deacon, so they would not have to wait on tables, and could focus on teaching and evangelising. Modern deacons do everything a priest does, except celebrate the Eucharist or Holy Communion. In smaller parishes, such as the one I was assigned to in rural Manitoba, deacons and licensed lay ministers, are often authorized to conduct a Holy Communion service using bread and wine already consecrated by a supervising priest. The ordination service in St. James Cathedral in Toronto was glorious. There was a full choir, fabulous music and a real sense of the presence of the Holy Spirit. As a candidate I had to kneel on a stone step for about ten minutes while the liturgy was sung and the prayers said. Figure 7.1 taken outside the Cathedral with my family shows the joy on our faces.

Figure 7.1: Ordination Day

7.2 Holland-Glenboro Parish in Manitoba

I was still discovering my new identity when we arrived in the tiny hamlet of Cyprus River (population 250). There had been a betrayal in the Diocese of Calgary. The Bishop met with Lucille and me one afternoon a month before graduation. After two drinks he had given us the crushing news that he had just filled all the vacancies, and there might not be a place for us in the Diocese of Calgary for a while. We later realized his priority was affirmative action for women priests, and the priest just appointed to where I could have gone was married to a female priest. As a Postulant of the Diocese, there was an assumption we would be returning and placed in a parish. The Bishop promised to bring us back, but first we had to commit to three years somewhere else. My ordination was uniquely complicated. It was for the Bishop of Brandon, by the Bishop of Toronto on the authority of the Bishop of Calgary. This betrayal of trust cost my family a great deal. We were separated from friends and grandparents at a critical time. My mother had died during my last year at Wycliffe and my father sadly died suddenly while we were in Manitoba. Perhaps the greatest cost was to the faith and spiritual life of our children, who learned that the Church can be just as political and corrupt as the world.

The good news always comes out of the bad news. We were able to have a very positive and rewarding experience of rural ministry that prepared me for the dozen interims I would complete later. Holland-Glenboro was a unique challenge. There were six small churches in tiny hamlets strung out along highways 2 and 3 South and East of Brandon. Congregations ranged from a dozen to over thirty. The prognosis was dismal. The towns were a remnant of a time when horses could only go about fifteen miles a day. Populations were declining as farms grew ever more mechanized and larger. One parishioner managed seven sections of wheat — seven square miles. The bottom line was that I would probably be the last full-time priest they could afford. My mission was to prepare for this by training local Lay Readers to provide ongoing leadership and volunteer ministry in these communities. I started out by encouraged existing Bible study groups in each town. These Bible Study groups soon got into more prayer intercession and pastoral care. Now they serve as house churches with visiting clergy. We had home services during the winter in Belmont, as they had a piano and room for everyone. Why would you want to spend a whole day heating a large church building up from -40 degrees for two hours on Sunday?

Bishop Harding was impressed at my progress and appointed

me chair of the Diocese Program and Planning Committee. He gave the committee a mandate to develop a five year strategic plan for the diocese. I did not have any training in strategic planning, but as a librarian, knew how to find information. I found some books which introduced me to SWOT analysis. Each parish in the diocese was invited to have a special meeting to discuss, and make a list of their internal Strengths and Weaknesses, and the Opportunities and Threats in their community. These lists were forwarded to the committee which met, copied them on yellow sticky notes, and arranged these in four groupings on a large blank wall.

Then we sat back and prayed for guidance. We watched the outline of the strategic plan emerge like wood floating to the surface of a pond. By drawing an arrow from the internal Strengths (what we were good at) toward the external Opportunities (what was needed),n the strategic direction was clear. This also identified the specific threats and weaknesses that we had to deal with. When the resulting Draft Strategic Plan was presented at Synod for a vote of approval, everyone just stood up and applauded. It was their plan, because all the information had come from them and they were all involved in drafting it. This process has been the key to my success in helping over a dozen parishes find an effective new direction for their ministry, as part of my interim ministry and consulting work.

I continued to discover my spiritual life as Father John through many challenging ministry experiences. One of the hardest was when one of the youngest and most spiritually alive women in the Glenboro Church was driving her daughter north to Carberry. As they were driving past a farm driveway, the axle on a front end loader suddenly broke. This turned the loader directly in front of the oncoming car, shearing off the car's roof. Mazo was killed instantly, and her daughter traumatized and in hospital. I was called and raced to the nearby farm where her husband Ron had just been given the news by the police. Everyone was in shock. All I could think of was to pray for help, as I held Ron and said "Just breathe in and breathe out." This tragedy brought the town together in a spectacular way. For the funeral they blocked off the main street, so we could put 200 extra chairs outside the church on the street and include everyone. At Communion time, we gave people Communion outside. It was a powerful spiritual experience of the love of Jesus reaching out to a community in grief.

Holland-Glenboro Parish was also a lesson in ecumenical relations. On Sunday the Lutheran pastor and I both had services in Glenboro at 9:00 AM. Then we both drove the 26 kilometres to Balder where the churches are across the street from each other. One Christmas, God challenged us. There was a big snowstorm at Devils Lake, North Dakota where the Lutheran pastor lived (no comment). He could not get to Baldur for the service, and called me to ask if we could invite the Lutherans to the Anglican service. This was a great idea, so we did and everyone had a wonderful experience. Baldur is a town of perhaps 200 people where they do everything together — except on Sunday. This went so well the pastor and I agreed to work with our leadership committees to have more joint services. Soon I was doing Lutheran services in the Lutheran Church and he was doing Anglican services in the Anglican Church. The services are almost identical, so we even tried me doing Lutheran services in the Anglican Church and him doing Anglican services in the Lutheran church.

This went well until I was invited to officiate at a huge baptism at the historic Lutheran church at Grund. We had a lot of visitors and they were crowding around the font taking pictures during the baptism. As baptism is a sacrament, I asked them to not take pictures during the sacrament and to move back so everyone could see. They were offended that I did not know that this was normal in a Lutheran Church, complained to their pastor, who complained to my bishop. I was called in and had to yet again explain the Matthew 18 dispute resolution procedure. This is the Christian rule about first going alone to the person who offended you for resolution, before involving others. It was all very sad as pride and unforgiveness was able to spoil a budding ecumenical relationship. I discovered too late, that sometimes you have to lose a battle graciously in order to win a war.

After three years in Manitoba I began applying for positions in Calgary Diocese. A year later I was still losing out to the bishop's political agenda of affirming women priests. Our daughter Mary started calling me after school because some of the children had threatened to beat her up on the way home. We met with the teachers and parents and tried to stop the bullying. When this failed, we knew it was time to come home to Alberta.

When the Bishop of Calgary found out I had given notice in Brandon Diocese, he immediately sent a disheartening letter saying he could not guarantee me a place in Calgary Diocese. We decided, for our daughter's sake, we would have to rescue ourselves. We moved back to Calgary at our own expense and I had to become a "worker priest" (like Jesus). It was a very difficult time spiritually, and emotionally humiliating to be on unemployment insurance with a wife, two young children and three university degrees. The good news was that we had already learned to trust God for financial provision when we started our consulting business "The Gishler Group: Library and Information System consultants in 1985.

7.3 The Gishler Group:
Learning To Trust God

One of the things we have discovered over the past 25 years is that when you are doing God's work in God's way, there is always adequate financial provision. We had some savings and a severance package after my position was terminated by the library board but being unemployed is always a traumatic and financially draining experience. We had two young children, including a daughter still on oxygen. There were a lot of bills to pay between the end of my library career in 1985 and employment as a priest in 1990. We were blessed then and many times since between interim ministry appointments, with provision from our new consulting business —

The Gishler Group: Library and Information System Consultants.

I discovered that my passion and gifts for helping people organize and find information as a librarian were transferrable to library and records management consulting. In Red Deer it was taking a long time to get a library job so like many others, I decided to hire myself. I had done economic consulting work briefly in Edmonton and contracted to establish a small departmental library in the Economics Department while a student at Western. I had lots of contacts in the business community, through membership in the Red Deer Rotary Club. Soon there was "Gishler Group: Library and Information System Consultants" letterhead and business cards. We were a "group" because Lucille, also a professionally qualified librarian, was my partner. Our 12 projects included:

- In Red Deer we started by developing a database of suppliers catalogues for an engineering company, a Band List database for the Montana Band and an engineering library for Novacor Chemicals/Alberta Gas Ethylene.
- In Toronto I developed a suppliers catalogue database for the Airports Authority Group of Transport Canada and a slide classification database for the YWCA.
- In Calgary we developed complete records management systems for the Calgary Foundation, Stony Tribal Administration, Builders Energy and Yukon Energy in Whitehorse.

One of the most interesting things we discovered was how many deeply spiritual people there are, who have given up on the Church or never found a nourishing church home. In each project we worked on we connected with a few men and women of deep faith. We could tell they were spiritual intuitively. Our personal spirits lifted when we were around them. Many had *Gone Spiritual* in spite of their negative church experiences. This was often as a result of personal Bible reading to find the something more of the Holy Spirit and a life of prayer and holiness. This taught me that Father John could be a worker priest (just like Jesus). Our Gishler Group projects kept us afloat financially in Red Deer, at Wycliffe College in Toronto and between interims when we returned to Calgary in

1995.

These consulting experiences prepared me for 25 years of exciting interim ministry where I had to work with church leaders and congregations to help them heal past wounds, find a vision and gently move the right people into leadership. Over the years the Gishler Group evolved from establishing library systems to paper Records Management systems and finally to electronic file management. As I was never a full-time incumbent in the Diocese of Calgary, our consulting work (fourteen projects total) kept food on the table. I enjoyed telling people that I was a "worker priest" — like Jesus.

Going Spiritual is a process of going from trusting in yourself, your family, friends and bank account; too trusting in God. We have Jesus' promise that "I am with you always" (in the form of the Holy Spirit). (Matthew 28.20, NIV) *Going Spiritual* is a gradual re-ordering of priorities, as your focus shifts from life limited to the physical dimension, to a new life in the invisible spiritual dimension that is lived in the physical dimension.

7.4 Interim Ministry in Alberta

My consulting experience in economics, libraries and records management was very good preparation for a more demanding and exciting opportunity to act temporarily as the spiritual father of many churches in Alberta. It was the religious equivalent of being the hired gun with the ability to go somewhere and solve a difficult problem. My business card read "Have Bible Will Travel." Older readers my remember the TV program *Have Gun, Will Travel*.

After we moved home to Calgary in 1995 I was able to re-train for proactive interim ministry. This built naturally on my consulting and strategic planning experience in Manitoba. I was blessed to father over a dozen churches through the often year-long gap between one priest leaving and another coming. In the Anglican tradition this can be a time of fear and drift. A trained interim priest can turn this drift into an opportunity to:

- Re-connect to the Diocese and begin the selection process
- Help the congregation come to terms with its history
- Review their spiritual priorities as a congregation and develop a strategic plan
- Develop congregational buy-in to the new plan
- Manage changes in leadership as new people step forward

Interims have a tremendous advantage over permanent clergy. Like a gunfighter in the old west, they know they are leaving and so they are politically free to challenge and heal difficult situations. They can confront and heal destructive parishioners, with tougher love than someone who is trying to develop long-term relationships. The interim ministry training course is an intensive four week retreat. This is followed by six months of field experience and then two more weeks in retreat to share learning.

I have found this to be very spiritually uplifting work. We are all trying to discern what Jesus and the Holy Spirit are trying to do in a particular community with specific people. As interim Priest, my primary job was to keep things running smoothly and provide worship leadership, teaching and pastoral support. This always included reaching out to everyone on the parish list, including those who had left. Many people have been wounded in their spiritual life by insensitive clergy and conflict in parishes. Interim ministry is an opportunity to reach out, particularly to people going through divorce, job loss and serious illness or death. These people need to experience the grace, love, forgiveness and healing they need for a rich spiritual life.

My interim ministry began formally at St. Cuthbert and St. George's in Sundre Alberta. This is a beautiful small Anglican church nestled in the foothills just West of Olds. They had been part of a declining four point rural parish. When the incumbent left, they had a bad experience with a priest who was not a trained interim. Ironically this was the woman who had been brought into the Diocese when I graduated. They wanted me to help them develop a lay-led model of team ministry and provide monthly clergy support. The priest would come to celebrate the Eucharist, consecrate extra bread and wine for distribution at a lay-led Communion services and provide some limited pastoral support and training. They pioneered in this as the only parish in the Diocese with a Lay Reader-in-Charge as opposed to the usual Priest-in-Charge. This has been working well for over twenty years. I have continued to be one of their support priests and a proud spiritual father of lay ministry for over 25 years.

This experience led to my next appointment as interim in Rimbey Alberta about an hour north. They had a similar problem where the shared incumbent had left, and the other town had decided they wanted to call a resident full-time priest. It was the classic town vs. country issue and we found a very creative solution. As we worked through the five steps of interim ministry it seemed impossible to either share a priest or hire someone on a half-time basis. Somebody noted that there was a small Lutheran church, a half hour away that was having the same problem. We made inquiries and soon the Rimbey Vestry (board) decided to go as a group and meet with the Lutheran board. By this point the Anglican and (Evangelical) Lutheran Churches of Canada were in full communion. This meant that any ordained Lutheran or Anglican priest could serve both congregations.

I remember the mood in the van on the way to that meeting. "Lutherans — they are so different, how can we work together, they are barely a liturgical church." But on the way home it was different: "they are interested in children, farm machinery and crops — just like us!" "They are not like town people who are interested in how their business is doing." "We like being with them." We all gathered after for a late night de-brief and (being Anglicans) a drink to celebrate. The Anglican/Lutheran parish of Rimbey — Bentley was born and I was the proud spiritual father.

From Rimbey I went to complete interims in Didsbury, then Olds and Didsbury and Olds together. These parishes were originally together under one priest but still resisted working together. I was told that in addition to the generic problem of local pride, another cause for these churches failure to thrive, is the presence of

Masonic lodges in these towns. This is where I first became aware of the destructive influence of Masons on the spiritual life of a church. In Chapter 12 on page 165, we will share our experiences in being delivered from Masonic curses and serious spiritual oppression. This is where the role of the priest as spiritual father/protector became very real to me.

One of my most interesting experiences was in serving both the Chinese Anglican Fellowship and Dinka Anglican Fellowship. The Chinese had come mostly from Hong Kong when independence from Great Britain was announced. Unlike many Chinese in Canada they spoke Cantonese instead of Mandarin. The services were led by a Lay Reader in Cantonese (which I do not understand). My role was to stand up and preach the sermon in English and then celebrate the Eucharist. When I finished my sermon one of the men would stand up and read the Cantonese translation. This meant I had to put the sermon up on the internet so it could be downloaded and translated before the service. This led me to develop my blog www.spirituallifeteaching.info which has now had over 62,000 page views. It now serves as a resource for clergy and lay leaders looking for sermon ideas and teachings on baptism, healing and the Anglican Church.

The Dinka congregation also held services in Dinka with me popping up to teach and celebrate the Eucharist. They were refugees from the South Sudan, the world's newest country, following a twenty-year civil war. Many in the congregation had grown up in refugee camps in Kenya so we had a special bond. I was privileged to mentor their Lay Reader through courses at Ambrose University to ordination as an Anglican priest.

My best interim experience was at St. George's in Calgary. I had discovered a new and more spiritual discernment process in *Moving Off The Map: A Field Guide to Changing the Congregation* by Thomas Bandy, a Canadian.[36] This process involved everyone in the congregation. There were nine discernment groups. Each met three or four times to go through an imaginary wagon train exercise, where they could only carry a small number of basic beliefs and core val-

Figure 7.2: Chinese Anglican Fellowship.

ues. Each group had to discuss and agree on their five or six basic beliefs and core values. In one heartbreaking meeting, they had to leave even two of these behind; to get across a "dangerous river." Each group reported the results at a congregational meeting. We had to again pray for wisdom, search our hearts, and agree on a final combined parish list of basic beliefs and core values. Next they had to meet again in small groups, and come up with a basic mission statement. This statement had to reflect the basic beliefs and core values, fit into an advertisement on the side of a bus, and explain what we were to do as a congregation. I was present when after prayer someone in our discernment group got what could only be a word of knowledge from the Lord:

> "To proclaim God's grace, love, forgiveness and healing to all God's children, in Jesus' Name."

Figure 7.3: St. George's, Calgary.

There was a long silence as the words washed over us. It was an awesome moment of truth. This statement was adopted by the next congregational meeting. In every service, in every church since then (2001), I dismiss the congregation with the same words:

> "Let us go forth in peace to proclaim God's grace, love, forgiveness and healing, to all God's children, in Jesus' Name."

This is probably a good summary of what all clergy should be saying to their congregation at the end of a worship service.

St. George's was the spiritual high point of my interim ministry.

The congregation were very involved in Cursillo, open to the gifts of the Holy Spirit and had a serious healing ministry. As is normal in an interim, I was invited to apply for the permanent position of incumbent. This is against the number one rule of interim ministry. By not being available as a candidate for the position (and having to "please" everyone) the interim priest is free to challenge destructive individuals who are blocking parish spiritual development. I had recently broken this rule, and then not been appointed to a parish. I rather hastily and without prayer said "no" to St. George's. Part of me wishes I had accepted their offer as our family would have finally had stability, and we could all have grown spiritually together. The upside of leaving was that I was able to serve in a wider variety of city, rural and international parishes:

- St. Mark's, Calgary
- Chinese Anglican Fellowship, Calgary
- Dinka Anglican Fellowship, Calgary
- St. Luke's, Calgary
- St. Magloire's, Drumheller
- St. George's, St. Vincent (our companion Diocese)
- St. Edmund's, Calgary

This variety of experience has taught me what makes churches thrive and help people develop and heal their spiritual lives. This story follows in Chapter 8 on the facing page and Chapter 9 on page 133.

Chapter 8

Developing a Spiritual Life

Spiritual life must be nourished and developed or it will weaken and die. If our personal spirit becomes polluted by our rebellion against God's law and feelings of guilt it weakens. A sin-polluted personal spirit may become so weak that it is unable to sustain our bodies, leading to sickness and eventually biological death. The good news of the Bible is that God has provided a way to both nourish our spiritual life and remove the spiritual pollution of sin-guilt through belief in Jesus Christ. Believers are promised the Holy Spirit will come to them and comfort, heal and guide them in developing their spiritual life. Believers are also promised that God will forgive sins if they are repented, confessed and taken in faith to the Cross of Jesus. This cleanses our spirit and makes it possible for the Holy Spirit to come and live inside us more fully. The Holy Spirit in turn helps us develop our spiritual life, by opening our spiritual eyes, and giving us the spiritual gifts of love, joy, peace, patience, longsuffering and wisdom. These gifts or fruits of the Holy Spirit are tangible evidence that our spiritual life is real. This evidence gives us hope that our personal spirit will be able to carry our soul to heaven when our body dies.

This is just the beginning. As we mature in our spiritual life, we discover our personal spiritual gifts:

"Now to each one the manifestation of the Spirit is given

for the common good. To one there is given through the Spirit a message of wisdom, to another a message of knowledge by means of the same Spirit, to another faith by the same Spirit, to another gifts of healing by that one Spirit, to another miraculous powers, to another prophecy, to another distinguishing between spirits, to another speaking in different kinds of tongues,[a] and to still another the interpretation of tongues. All these are the work of one and the same Spirit, and he distributes them to each one, just as he determines." (1 Corinthians 7-11)

This is where our spiritual life becomes truly awesome! It is also where our religious and social life becomes complicated and challenging. The challenge is that we live in relationship with other people who may not have had the same awesome experiences. If everyone around us were emotionally secure and perfectly loving it would be ok. The reality is that they are not, and may respond with fear. Fearful minds go for the negative. Are you more of a Christian because you pray in tongues? Am I a failure because I do not? The gift of tongues has always been divisive in the Church.

> "And these signs will accompany those who believe: In my name they will drive out demons, they will speak in new tongues,…" (Mark 16-17)
>
> "All of them were filled with the Holy Spirit and began to speak in other tongues as the Spirit enabled them." (Acts 2.4)
>
> "Therefore, my brothers and sisters, be eager to prophesy, and do not forbid speaking in tongues. (1 Corinthians 14.39)"

The evidence of this divisiveness is all around us. Pentecostal churches, named after the birth of the Church at Pentecost, have had to separate from the mainline churches to avoid conflict.

My own experiences of the Holy Spirit and the gifts of the spirit (words of knowledge, teaching, healing, prophecy and recently tongues), has made me feel uncomfortable in churches where these gifts are discouraged or rarely talked about. We experienced this experience gap recently when I asked my former professor at Wycliffe College about the courses he was developing in Gambia, West Africa. I told him about Charles Kraft going to West Africa as a missionary. The local people came to him for deliverance from evil spirits, then went back to the witch doctors when he could not help them. This was apparently new information to my former teacher. He was more excited about teaching Hebrew in Gambia.

The most difficult part of developing a spiritual life is finding a local church community which can provide a healthy balance of authentic Bible teaching, experiences of the Holy Spirit, emotional encouragement and a meaningful purpose. It is arrogant and foolish to think we can discover, develop and heal our spiritual life outside of a nurturing church community.

As a cradle Anglican I have been nourished by Bible reading, teaching, worship, and the sacraments of baptism, confession and holy communion. I enjoy the gasps in some Anglican churches when somewhere in a sermon I wake everyone up, by sharing that I was a cradle Anglican until I went through a divorce crisis, read the whole Bible myself, experienced the Holy Spirit, and became a serious Christian. There is always a great deal of sucking in of air, and whispers about whether or not I said what I just said. The implication is that they probably have not yet "got it." They too may need to read the whole Bible and experience the Holy Spirit to become a serious Christian.

It is a challenge to go deeper in Bible study and prayer for the gifts of the Holy Spirit in developing their spiritual lives.

My Bible reading experience was followed by a short time when I was a bit like one of those Bible thumping evangelicals on TV. Extreme evangelicals often fall into the religious trap of the Biblical Pharisees. They know all about the law of God, but not about the love of God. This is the trap of a Religious spirit of judgement, for which I later had healing. Like many former evangelicals I was emotionally and spiritually starving in this environment.

Then I was drawn to the love and sense of community of more theologically liberal churches. My time as a theological liberal was short lived. Their long theological debates over same-sex blessings and marriage pushed me back toward what I consider a more healthy theological balance between the law of God and the love of God. The key to developing a healthy Christian spiritual life is finding a nurturing church that balances community, orthodoxy, relevance and outreach.

In 1993, two years after ordination, I was able to attend a workshop on church growth in Toronto which examined both why Canadians leave churches — and what are the criteria of a spiritually thriving church in Canada. The workshop was led by Don Posterski, who worked with Irwin Barker of the polling firm Angus Reid to develop and conduct statistically reliable research on effective Protestant churches in Canada.[37] They used 26 focus groups across the country to test survey questions. Next they conducted a statistically rigorous survey of Canadians in thriving churches, to determine what they like about their churches, what would justify them leaving a church and what they would look for in a new church. The survey results, based on 761 returned responses from lay people, clergy and academics, identified the four pillars of an effective (i.e., spiritually nourishing) church as:

- Community
- Orthodoxy
- Relevance
- Outreach

These are the four pillars of effective churches that help people develop a healthy and serious spiritual life. I have been trying to help churches develop strength and balance in these areas during my twenty-five years of ordained ministry in Manitoba and Alberta. Understanding these four signs of a thriving church will help you find a church community where your spiritual life can be nourished and developed.

8.1 Community:
In Touch with Personal Needs

In 2016 I made a very interesting discovery. After 25 years of serving in over a dozen Anglican parishes in Manitoba and Alberta, I was burned out. I was 74 and it was time to become a little more semi-retired. We had recently completed two challenging interims, an overseas mission and a healing mission. I needed to just sit in a pew and be spiritually nourished. Since Lucille had faithfully followed me from church to church for over thirty years, it was more than time for her to choose a church. We did what you have to do to find a good church. You have to get out and bump around till you find it. Staying at home and sulking is spiritually destructive and gets you nowhere.

After bumping around a few other churches, we decided we should try Christ Church, Calgary. This should not have been hard. We knew several people there and have listened to a CD of their magnificent choir every morning for the last 10 years while having breakfast. This was a big challenge for me. They have had a history of very theologically liberal clergy and were about to get another. On our first Sunday I was praying for a sign that this would be ok. As we walked in we were handed a leaflet and a ticket for a draw which I put in my pocket. After the service we walked into the coffee area just as they were calling out some numbers for the draw. I heard them call out "762." I looked in my pocket for my ticket, read the number 762, and held it up as I claimed my prize! It was a three-day pass to the Welsh Music festival in Calgary. This was a good sign!

The next week I came prepared with an idea from the Alpha Course Leaders Training video. Nicky Gumbel, who developed the Alpha Course, shared his first experience of the Anglican Church in England as a young man. He had attended a Bible study, asked a question and was riding home on this bicycle, pondering the priest's answer. The priest (a Ph.D.), had responded "That's very interesting. Nobody has ever asked that question before. Let me think about it till next week." Nicky was so proud of himself. Imagine, he who had never read the Bible or attended church, had asked a theological question this highly educated priest had never heard before. Nicky wondered if he had found his gift. Perhaps he should become a priest? As he continued peddling, another thought entered his mind — "or …that was the dumbest question anyone ever asked, and the priest did not want to embarrass him." I resolved that no matter how offensive the teaching I was going to smile and only think and say "that's very interesting."

Sure enough the main point of the next sermon at Christ Church turned out to be not about the faith example of the Centurion (as the text says), but the BIBLICAL FACT, that he was of course in a homosexual relationship with his servant "whom he loved." I felt the hair rise on my neck. Then I calmed down, smiled to myself and thought to myself "that's very interesting I have never heard that before."

What I learned during our first few weeks was that community may be just as important as orthodoxy in nourishing spiritual life. From the moment we walked into this Church, we felt at home. We already knew half a dozen people at coffee time, and every Sunday were introduced to more. What is most important is that we sensed they were our kind of people. They were well educated, interesting to talk to, successful in business and professions, well travelled and caring about people. This was warm (spiritually nourishing) love as opposed to the cold love we had often experienced in more evangelical churches. We had found a community where our emotional needs were being met. This is consistent with what Posterski found in his survey of what people in effective Canadian churches wanted:[38]

- 82% Sense of belonging
- 70% Building self worth
- 69% Opportunity for involvement
- 60 % Emphasis on family
- 50% Meeting emotional needs

My best experiences of serious Christian community have been on Cursillo weekends. My Cursillo experience transformed my life as described above. For three days I was surrounded by a deep sense of Christian love and fellowship. This is what our heart, our personal spirit, needs to develop and grow.

We have also found community attending and leading the 12 week Alpha Course several times. We developed a deep bond of community with the Alpha Course Students, and with the Bible Study and Prayer groups at St. George's Cathedral on St. Vincent, during our five month mission. They are the happy people on the steps of the Anglican Pastoral Centre on St. Vincent in Figure 8.1. This was a deeper spiritual bond than we have felt in some Canadian churches.

Figure 8.1: St. Vincent Alpha Course.

My sense is that most people in our Canadian culture are not really happy. My suspicion is that a significant reason for this is that they are emotionally empty and lonely inside. They do not have a spiritual life in the sense of a deep emotional relationship with other people and Jesus Christ. They are hungry for an authentic experience of Christian community.

8.2 Orthodoxy:
In Touch with the Truth

One of our baptismal promises in the Anglican Church is to remain in the Apostolic teaching and the fellowship. Orthodoxy may be defined as teachings consistent with the earliest and most reliable Hebrew and Greek texts of the Bible. Many people do not realize how much reliable and consistent information is available. There are over 6,000 fragments and copies of books and letters, some as early as 300 AD. I have seen a fragment of a copy of Paul's Letter to the church in Philippi, dated from 330 AD, in the British Library. There is more physical evidence available for the man Jesus than for Julius Caesar.

The Acts of the Apostles and letters of the Apostle Paul date from the First Century. They remind us that conflicts over doctrine and with false teachers were the norm. Most of the earliest church leaders died for their faith. False teaching was to be resisted at all costs, including torture and death. Anglican clergy must publicly sign a statement that they believe the Scriptures of the Old and New Testament contain everything needed for salvation before ordination. "… Do not go beyond what is written…" (1 Corinthians 4:6) Any new prophecy or teaching that is contrary to the clear meaning of the Bible is by definition heretical — even if approved by a pope, church council or synod.

Orthodoxy is the good news of the Bible that Jesus Christ came into this world to save sinners through faith in His sacrificial death on the Cross as a way to forgiveness of sins, and an eternal spiritual life of joy. Jesus mission statement in Luke 4.18-19 describes exactly what Christians are to do in following His example:

- Be anointed by the Holy Spirit to **preach** this good news to the poor (those who don't have), so they can
- **Proclaim** freedom for the prisoners (including those imprisoned in false teachings), which leads to
- **Recovery** of sight for the blind (spiritually as well as physically), which leads to the
- **Release the oppressed** (spiritually and politically)
- To **proclaim** the year of the Lord's favour (God's blessings)

The purpose of being anointed by the Holy Spirit is to proclaim boldly and with authority. Proclaim is a verb, an action word, that suggests an aggressive proclamation of the truth. This is what people are seeking and what they need to hear, to develop and nourish their spiritual life. Jesus taught "Blessed are those who are persecuted because of righteousness, for theirs is the kingdom of heaven." Remaining silent in the face of opposition to orthodoxy (political correctness) is not really an option.

Jesus' Mission Statement teaches us we have to be serious, not dabblers, in our spiritual life. The purpose of preaching the good news is to proclaim freedom for prisoners. Proclaim is not a suggestion or a hope. Proclaim means we must (not may) try to free people who are imprisoned physically, mentally and spiritually. Jesus spend a great deal of his time proclaiming the good news of the Kingdom of God to free the Pharisees. They had imprisoned themselves and others in a rigid religious practice of 615 teachings or regulations related to keeping the Ten Commandments. The bottom line was that the Pharisees, like some modern teachers, were guilty of idolatry because they were honouring their interpretation of the Law, more than the Law-giver (God).

Powerful preaching and proclamation leads to opening blind eyes. Some people are physically blind and Jesus was able to heal them. But many more of the people Jesus talked to, were spiritually blind. They were blinded by false and obscure Hebrew teachings and could not see the truth about God.

The physically imprisoned may need to "see" the error of their ways, repent and change their ways before they become spiritually freed. The mentally and spiritually imprisoned (see strongholds above) may need to see the truth about God, repent and renounce false doctrines to become free.

When Jesus talks about the oppressed, he is not just thinking of the Roman occupation. As we "go spiritual," our spiritual eyes are opened and we see a whole new level of meaning in the Bible. We see that Jesus is often talking about the spiritual, not the material aspects of life. The oppressed in the mission statement include not just the poor and the politically oppressed. Some people are oppressed spiritually by demons and evil spirits. This is what many people discover as they develop their spiritual life through healing experiences as described in Chapter 12 on page 165.

This mission statement is a timeless prophecy of God's plan of salvation (from Isaiah 42.7, 49.8-9, 58.6). The orthodox text we are to proclaim is in writing. The consistency of theology through all the 66 biblical books, written by different people in different countries between 550 BC and 200 AD, could only be achieved by the inspiration of a single divine author. Posterski found that this orthodoxy is an essential characteristic of an effective church that helps people develop a spiritual life:

> "In the midst of Canadian pluralism and increased secularization, the people of God do not want to attend worship and hear sermons that dismantle the foundations of their basic beliefs. Instead, they view strong preaching and sound doctrinal teaching as an essential characteristic of an effective church."[39]

Posterski wisely asked this key question on orthodoxy from a negative point of view, to ensure respondents answered more truthfully. Two thirds disagreed with the statement "It is very difficult for churches to relate to the outside world without compromising their traditional Biblical teaching."[40] Unfortunately, this compromising of traditional biblical teachings to be more relevant to society, describes perfectly the theological direction and strategy of many Protestant churches in Canada over the last 50 years.

I first became aware of this modern decline in orthodox teaching through Pierre Burton's *The Comfortable Pew: A Critical Look At the Church in the New Age*, published in 1965. Burton criticized the Canadian Protestant churches (he was Anglican), for trying to adapt Christianity to the culture to maintain the privileges and prestige of the bishops; instead of challenging the secular culture with the radical Christian Faith of the Bible. Sadly our stronghold-blinded Anglican and Lutheran bishops failed to hear this warning (see self-deception and strongholds above) and continued down the politically correct path of deconstructing the authority of the Bible. The consequences of this decline in orthodoxy has been a steep decline in church attendance in direct proportion to the degree of unorthodox teaching over the last 50 years:

- Roman Catholic (most orthodox) down 20%
- Anglican (Episcopal) down 40%
- United Church of Canada (least orthodox) down 60%

In the absence of orthodox Christian proclamation in many of our churches, our North American culture has degenerated into a post-Christendom, and now "post-truth" society. Instead of determining orthodoxy or truth through the clash of serious ideas and rigorous debate, conflict is avoided by the haze of liberal respectfulness. This requires a mind boggling (self-deceiving) acceptance of ideas on both sides of a debate as equally true. Opinion has been elevated to the status of truth, without the traditional checks and balances to weed out misguided opinions. Now, avoiding intelligent debate and conflict is sadly, more important than truth.

We seem to be living in a narcissistic anti-truth culture of self-deception. This is very confusing for everyone, and very destructive to orthodoxy and the development of spiritual life. Going back to my childhood tree house story, it seems like the "tree house" of Christendom has been dismantled, and now we are discovering that the theological liberals, like my childhood friend, were lying when they said they knew how to build a better one.

8.3 Relevance:
In Touch with the Times

Not accommodating the culture does not mean not trying to understand it. Posterski found that 53% of respondents thought understanding the culture was "very important."[41] Churches that become a holy huddle, for protection against pagan outsiders, soon become irrelevant cliques. Effective churches that nourish spiritual life have a balance between the four pillars of community, orthodoxy, relevance and outreach. Relevance is about being in touch with the times: knowing where people are in their hopes, fears and needs. What people need is exactly what Jesus offered:

- Teaching that opens their spiritual eyes and leads to the recovery of their true identity and purpose as beloved children of God and signs of His glory in the world.
- Teaching and healing experiences that give freedom from the mental and spiritual prisons of false teachings, sin, guilt, shame and un-forgiveness.
- Teaching that explains why things go wrong and how things really work in this life and in the spiritual dimension.

People need a genuine personal experience of the Risen Jesus through the Holy Spirit. This experience is what makes Jesus relevant and opens their spiritual eyes to the possibility of forgiveness, healing and an eternal spiritual life of joy.

Many people in our time are confused. Their lives seem to be without purpose or meaning. We seem to be living in a time that is between times. Christendom and the shared values of an older generation have been largely replaced in Western cultures by a vague new progressive liberalism (a stronghold). This liberal progressivism knows what it is against – Christian moral teachings that limit their sex lives. But it has no clear meaning or purpose beyond vague platitudes about love, inclusion and freedom. I am reminded of my tree house experience in Chapter 3 on page 26. I had just built a very nice tree house in our back yard in Ottawa. A friend was jealous and said he had an idea for an even better tree house. The problem was that we had to dismantle the one I had just built before we could build his better tree house. When the original tree house was dismantled, he grinned at me and admitted he did not really have a better idea.

My sense is that this is where progressivism and liberalism have taken western culture. They do not really have a better tree house or better set of religious or philosophical beliefs that give people in our culture meaning and purpose. The legacy of liberalism is the destruction of what has stood the test of time and created our great progressive Western civilizations. You can see the unhappy result all around in sad faces, addictions, broken marriages and stress, as people try to find happiness in drugs, alcohol, material possessions and sex (the deception of false love). Many of the those who came to us for healing ministry had lost their real identity as beautiful children of God. The culturally relevant issues that people need Christian teaching on and healing ministry for are:

- Anger
- Un-forgiveness (the only un-forgivable sin)
- Sin-guilt
- Sexual immorality and abuse (it's rampant)
- Personal identity theft (I am no good, a mistake, unlovable)
- Addictions (Alcoholism, Materialism, Sex, Power and Control)
- Truth and lying as murder of the truth
- Spiritual oppression, cults, pagan religions and idolatry

All of these things devastate lives and spiritual lives in particular but are rarely mentioned in sermons, at least in churches I attended for over 50 years. Many of these churches seemed to be on auto-pilot. They were declining because they had failed to see the danger and challenge the liberal destruction of biblical values. They were not offering orthodox teaching and healing that was relevant to people's lives. They were not helping people develop spiritual lives.

Posterski found that 85% of the people in effective churches agreed with the statement that "a church is not worth attending unless it provides practical guidance for expressing one's faith in the world during the week."[42] Christians that work in challenging environments need the support and guidance of a spiritual church community. They need regular nourishment in the form of shared stories and personal experiences of the Holy Spirit, and relevant biblical teaching. This means a church where the preaching helps them come to know and experience Jesus personally. They need to know how to connect their experiences of prayer and the Holy Spirit to their daily lives. They need practical as opposed to vague, intellectual religious teaching.

My own spiritual life developed from a combination of reading the Bible and praying at home daily, studying and attending healing ministry workshops and then having relevant experiences of the Holy Spirit and healing. I found relevance as people shared their faith experiences in church fellowship groups. Bible study and prayer groups always lead to the development of trust and sharing of life experiences. The Alpha Course and Cursillo Weekends are specifically designed to teach people how to share practical experiences of the Holy Spirit helping them in their daily lives. After 12 weeks of meeting for intimate sharing, everyone on an Alpha Course knows, trusts and misses the group if it ends. Cursillo is organized as a network of people who are "grouping" in small groups every two weeks to be accountable for their study, piety and action. The Weekend is designed to prepare people for this grouping. The monthly "Ultreya" is a gathering of the whole community for more sharing and fellowship.

One of the best ways churches can be relevant and help people go spiritual in the workplace is through dealing with difficult social issues in their sermon times. Posterski found that 26% of respondents thought it was important for churches to be open to talking about tough social issues.[43] Churches often have to choose between "going political" — affirming what is popular; and *Going Spiritual* — proclaiming the deep truths of Biblical wisdom. I often find it refreshing to attend the more evangelical churches, which seem to know where they stand on abortion, sexual confusion and marriage.

The New Wine (Alpha) churches in England and largest evangelical churches in Calgary and Vancouver are crowded with hundreds of young people at multiple services on Sundays. Young people are starving for relevant spiritual teaching and experiences that will help them develop a spiritual life in a post-truth culture.

In our time we have the strange paradox of many confused people who want to be spiritual but not religious. Many have been blinded by the mental strongholds of liberalism, homosexuality and progressivism. They are often the ones exploring Buddhism, Hinduism, Yoga and Islam. They want to get away from the irrelevant academic and political conflicts in Christian churches. They want to find relevant and authentic experiences of spiritual love, joy, peace and happiness. My heart breaks when they talk excitedly about having meaningful religious or even supernatural experiences in pagan religions. The bad news is that Satan can counterfeit the gifts of the Holy Spirit and deceive people like Siddhartha, Mohamed and me (see above) who are searching for a personal experience of God.

8.4 Outreach:
In Touch with the Needs of Others

Outreach is the work of God and the basic mission of the Church. The Bible begins with the Creation story and then continues for about 4,000 years of the history (His story), the story of God reaching out to different men and women in different times and places including:
- To Noah to save human life from destruction by a flood
- To Abraham to leave his home in Iraq and form a holy people
- To Moses to rescue those people from Egypt
- To Kings Solomon and David to form a holy nation
- As Jesus, His only begotten Son, to give up His life to redeem His people
- To Luther and later teachers and prophets to guide His people

Throughout this history the message and mission has been the same: to reach out and tell all people that God loves them, and to bring them into a holy covenant relationship of faith and love. This work of outreach is what gives the church community its relevance, meaning and purpose. Outreach nourishes people by bringing meaning and purpose to their lives. Many people are emotionally wounded, lonely, discouraged, sad and depressed because their lives do not have this sense of meaning and purpose. They are the poor (in spiritual life) that Jesus came to proclaim the good news to. This good news opens spiritual eyes, so people can see and understand the truth about God reaching out to them. This truth frees people from the mental prisons of fear, depression, hopelessness and ignorance about God, Jesus and the Holy Spirit. This truth frees people from false identities such as being "a failure," "not wanted" or the "wrong sex." The good news of God, Jesus and the Holy Spirit gives people new hope and joy.

When Lucille and I pray daily for all the members of our families, we pray that they will find some spiritual meaning and purpose for their lives. This is the most difficult challenge in life because our lives are filled with distractions, we have an enemy (Satan) and God has given us complete freedom to accept or reject His outreach of love.

Posterski found that "...70% of Christians surveyed rated 'a strong commitment to local evangelism' as a high priority in selecting a church to attend."[44] In what will be news to evangelicals, this interest in evangelization was not primarily for numerical growth. Sixty-two percent of respondents thought numerical growth was "not important."[45] Rather this work of outreach needs to be motivated by the internal needs of the community, for orthodoxy and relevance. Outreach is also a natural part of the Christian concern for social justice. "Three-quarters of Christians... felt that effective churches will address social problems like domestic violence, child abuse and racism from the pulpit."[46] What makes churches effective, and leads to personal spiritual growth, is the careful balance between these pliers of orthodoxy, community, relevance and outreach.

Figure 8.2 illustrates how some churches become out of balance and fail to provide a healthy nourishing environment for developing a spiritual life. The horizontal axis illustrate the tension between the inward focussed St. Worship's which is over emphasizing community but may be irrelevant to the culture, and St. Works' which is over emphasizing outward focussed works of love, possibly without much orthodoxy or sense of community.

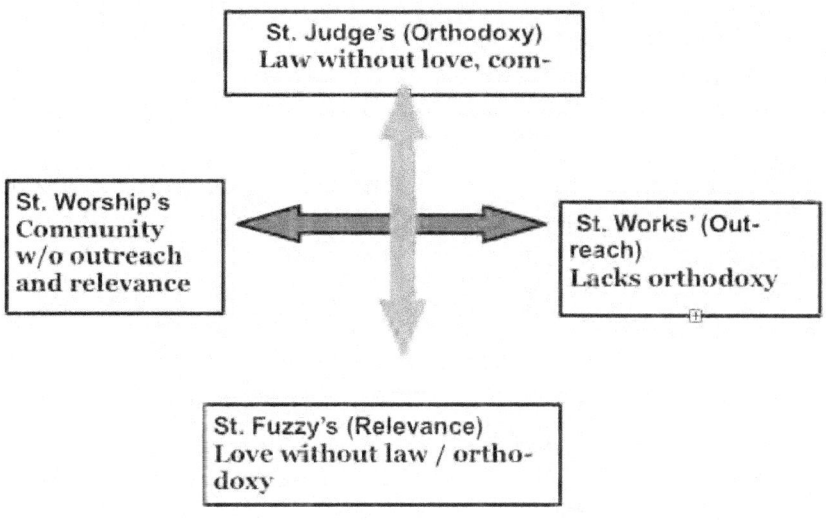

Figure 8.2

The vertical axis illustrates the tension between St. Fuzzy's which is over-emphasizing relevance to the culture and love, and St. Judge's which is over-emphasizing orthodoxy and God's law.

All four of these extreme churches are seriously out of balance and limited in terms of helping people develop a spiritual life:

I use this model to help church leaders visualize where their community is now and see if their community is centred or out of balance. I explain the four pillars as above and then hand out a the diagram and ask them to mark an X to indicate where they are on

the vertical and horizontal axis:
1. Draw an X where you think your church is along the left — right axis of the inward vs. outward focus of your church.
2. Draw another X along the up — down axis to show your church leadership where you think they are now in terms of being in touch with God vs. the local culture.
3. The distance from the mid-point of balance among these two tensions indicates how out of balance the church may be, and which direction the church may need to move in, to be more effective in helping people develop their spiritual lives.

Going Spiritual is a lifelong process of discovering, developing and healing our personal spiritual life. I have shared my own discoveries and how I developed my spiritual life by finding loving church communities that gave me emotional support, orthodox teaching, and opportunities to experience relevant outreach to the culture. Now it is time to dive a little deeper and share how my experiences of healing ministry helped me overcome the emotional and spiritual wounds of a lifetime and go much deeper in developing my spiritual life. Much of what follows may be completely new information for some readers. I ask you to read this with an inquiring mind and prayer for spiritual confirmation.

Part II
Healing Spiritual Life

Chapter 9

Wounds, Oppression, and Bondages/Strongholds

As I begin to discover and grow my spiritual life in a nourishing church community, I begin to realize how spiritually wounded I was. We are all spiritually wounded. In twenty five years of ordained ministry, I have never met anyone who did not need a great deal of healing prayer. Unfortunately, many people are not aware of their spiritual wounds. They are stuck, like I was; and unable to really figure out why they are so unhappy, and why things go wrong. In this chapter I share what learned from many spiritual directors, counsellors and people in the healing ministry between 1985 and 2017.

Going Spiritual is a learning experiencing and healing process, as we discover and seek healing for ever deeper layers of wounding that are polluting or distorting our spiritual life. Our spiritual wounding affects the invisible struggle going on in our soul between the holy desires of our personal spirit, and the worldly and sometimes destructive desires, of our ego and body as explained in Chapter 2 on page 9. Healing ministry helps by identifying and healing spiritual wounds, and freeing us from the oppression of sin-guilt. This creates a holy place in our personal spirit. The Holy Spirit can then come more fully to guide us and strengthen us from the inside. This helps us in overcoming the fleshly or sinful temptations of the world. This growing dominance of the human will by our spirit, through a holy relationship with God; is what we mean by going spiritual/being saved/becoming a serious Holy Spirit led Christian.

Our relationship with God is defined by our baptismal covenant. A covenant is a very special type of relationship that has powerful spiritual consequences if it is broken. Covenant relationship is what makes a Christian marriage, with Jesus as a party to the covenant, much more than a legal contract between two people. In baptism, Christians promise to love God and keep His commandments. This includes all the revealed teachings from the Ten Commandments, to the commandment of Jesus to love one another. There is no "wiggle room." Any failure to love and obey God, ourselves (God's creation) and others, is sinful. Sin is a rebellion against God that breaks our baptismal covenant and makes us unholy, and not able to be in the presence of God, who is holy. The good news is that God has provided a way to forgiveness and restoration to covenant relationship, through faith in the sacrificial death and resurrection of Jesus, for the sins of believers. God's part of the covenant is spiritual protection, and the promise to love and bless us with the gifts of the Holy Spirit. This is why sin is serious and can lead to spiritual wounds or even spiritual bondages.

If we do not repent and ask for forgiveness from our sins, they can become spiritual wounds. Spiritual wounds can open doorways for demons and spiritual attack. This, in turn, allows spiritual oppression from the inside, which is more powerful. If our spiritual wounds are not healed, they will continue to pollute the personal spirit, and hinder the development of spiritual life. The downward spiral of spiritual life may then continue, as selfish and destructive desires dominate the will, and continue to pollute the spiritual life. As we will see in the following healing stories, wounds can act as doorways for evil spirits which can deceive and oppress us from the inside as strongholds. This spiritual oppression may increase and lead to spiritual bondage (alcoholism, liberalism) and ultimately spiritual death. The physical body will live on; but when

Sins ➡ Wounds ➡ Oppression

➡ Bondages / Strongholds

Figure 9.1

it dies, the person may not have a spiritual life to live on in heaven.

This is why Satan could deceive Eve in the Garden Story with the words "You will not certainly die…" (Gen. 3.4). Her rebellion would cause her spirit to die, or begin dying, but her body would live on for a while. Healing our spiritual life, nourishing our spiritual life and protecting our spiritual life ensures we do not die, but live on spiritually in Heaven when our body dies. Having seen a vision of my late daughter Mary after death, I can assure you it is a glorious experience. We begin to experience this joy in our spirit in this life, but it gets better in the next. What people experience tangibly in healing ministry, is freedom from the bondage of past sin-guilt and an assurance that they are included in God's Kingdom on Earth and in heaven. Healing is an essential preparation for our spiritual life both here and in the Heavenly Kingdom.

My own experience of doing healing prayer came after Lucille had given me Catherine Marshall's classic book, *Something More*. This book explains Catherine Marshall's history of wrestling with the problem of depression, and her frustration that God did not seem to be responding to her prayers for healing. She became desperate enough to verbally acknowledge God's sovereignty through praise and thanksgiving, and depend on the Holy Spirit for healing.

My son Christopher was visiting from his home in London Ontario and sleeping in the bedroom. Lucille and I were talking in the living room when Christopher suddenly had a night terror. He started screaming and yelling. His mother had warned me it was very difficult to wake him and get him to stop. I had been reading in the Bible about taking authority over evil. We went into the bedroom, climbed up on the bed, put our hands on his head. Lucille prayed that the love of Jesus would flow through him and the moaning would stop. I took authority in the name of Jesus and said "Stop." It was really simple. What stunned us both was that it worked. It was like turning off a light switch. The screaming stopped instantly and Christopher continued to sleep peacefully. God's healing ministry through me had begun. Over the last 35 years we have been blessed and helped by the teaching of John and Paula Sandford, Tuk Su Koo, Wholeness through Christ, The International Order of St. Luke, Dr. Charles Kraft, Family Foundations International and our Blessings Fellowship of intercessors.

In this chapter I will share my experiences in receiving healing for my own spiritual wounds and praying for the healing of others. These stories are organized to illustrate first of all how people's spirits can become wounded and how these wounds can be healed through the intervention of the Holy Spirit in revealing the original sin and taking this to the Cross of Jesus for forgiveness and healing. Figure 9.2, based on the teachings of *Wholeness Through Christ*,[47] illustrates the general pattern of un-forgiven sin-guilt leading to wounds, then spiritual oppression and finally spiritual bondage or strongholds. Most healing ministry involves identifying the sin-guilt or emotional cause of the wound, and reversing this process through the self-examination, repentance, confession and absolution process. The goal is sins forgiven, wounds healed, spiritual oppression lifted and bondages broken.

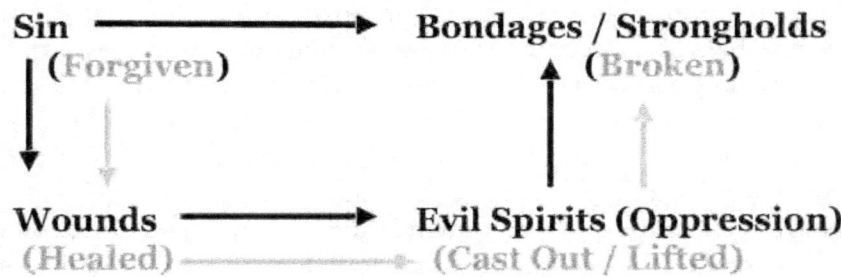

Figure 9.2

My own experiences of healing based on this model were profound. A prayer of forgetfulness is said after the ministry to cleanse both the ministers and counselee from spiritual pollution. These workshops are very powerful because while the team of three is praying, there is also a room full of other participants holding them up in prayer. The ministry session lasts for at least an hour. The ministry team includes three people. The most experienced one takes the lead and is held up in prayer by number two. The third member acts as a scribe. My sin roots were not very surprising: the usual anger, pride, judgement, lust, idolatry and un-forgiveness. These had led predictably to bondages or strongholds of perfectionism and judgementallism. What was new to me was the continuing reality of my emotional wounds. These could be traced back to a painful birth (my mother had mentioned this several times), lack of intimacy with parents as a child, the trauma of a divorce and the loss of relationship with my son. The combination of these sins and wounds, had led predictably to bondages of anger, un-forgiveness, perfectionism, jugementallism and a religious spirit.

These bondages are often easy to spot — except for the religious spirit. This is the bondage or religious stronghold of the Pharisees. They were proud of thinking they knew, better than anyone else, including Jesus, what God wanted. This is a terrible bondage because it constitutes spiritual pride, and focuses on intellectual knowledge of God, and away from personal experience and a real love relationship with Jesus. This is what drives the cold love found in many evangelical churches. It drives emotionally sensitive Christians out of these churches and into more theologically liberal and loving churches. The danger of this is that these wounded people may not get orthodox teaching and may become seduced by extreme liberal theology. I have been back and forth between these two extremes of law without love, and love without law, myself. The good news is that as a result of humbling myself, repenting, and seeking forgiveness from Jesus, the spiritual power of these bondages has been broken. I am still working on my behaviour habits.

My most vivid memory of the Wholeness Through Christ ministry is of a vision where I was first in a horse corral with Jesus trying to comfort me. We then sat across a large round table and had a beer together. Then we went for a walk in heaven where I could see a long corridor or wall made of shining gold. It got brighter and brighter until I was simply bathed in light. I assume this was the heavenly throne room and presence of God but all I could see was light. After the healing session, when Lucille and I went up to our room, my face was visibly glowing; presumably like that of Moses after his meeting with God on Mount Sinai. (Exodus 34.29-30)

Chapter 10

Healing Wounds From Trauma

Our personal spirit is very sensitive and fragile. It senses the emotional pain in our minds and the physical pain of our bodies. As our intuitive sensor, our spirit it also senses the emotional and physical pain of those we know and love. This makes counselling and healing ministry emotionally draining. We must depend on the Holy Spirit working through our bodies for healing, or like many counsellors we will become y burned out after twenty years. Our ministry self-care included prayers of forgetfulness so the details are long forgotten. Self protection should also include taking a spiritual shower of praise music to wash away the pollution, physical rest and prayer coverage by experienced healers. The story of our daughter Mary is traumatizing so you will need to start your self-care before reading this.

Emotional or physical trauma, including major illness has an invisible effect on our personal spirit. It is not the trauma, but how we react to the trauma event, that does the spiritual damage. For example Lucille was born with her umbilical cord wrapped around her neck. Her tiny spirit would have been very afraid of death. Her natural reaction of fear, the opposite of love, wounded her spirit. In turn, this wound acted as a doorway for a spirit of fear, to enter and oppress her for many years before being cast out. The birth of Mary challenged us to cry out to Jesus and the Holy Spirit for healing, and pushed us deep into prayer ministry. The Holy Spirit did show up and saved Mary's life. But physical and spiritual damage had been done, and continued to be done as Mary suffered physical pain (needles), emotional trauma and damage to her short term memory. This is a story of love, courage and healing, as Mary struggled for 24 years to recover from these wounds through the love of her family, medical care and a great deal of prayer ministry.

10.1 The Birth, Life and Death of Mary

The birth of our precious daughter Mary in 1984 taught me to love unconditionally and got Lucille and me into a deep and serious healing ministry. Lucille was 39 and past her best-before childbearing years. Our son David, born 14 months earlier, had also been a "high-risk" pregnancy with Lucille on bed rest for three months before his birth. She was now under the watchful eye of the High Risk Pregnancy Team in Calgary. I had been passed over for a promotion at the Calgary Public Library because the Board wanted to promote a woman. When the Director of the Red Deer Public Library retired and the position was advertised, this seemed to be a great opportunity. I applied, was interviewed and offered the position. The problem was that Red Deer was a small city 125 km north of Calgary. In the biggest mistake of my life, I put my career ahead of my responsibilities as a husband, refused to consider commuting, staying over, and pressured Lucille into moving.

There was a large Regional hospital in Red Deer, and one of my best friends from university in Edmonton was a respected family physician there — but there was no High Risk Pregnancy Team. To not confuse social and professional relationships, Lucille decided to choose another doctor. This did not go well. After one of her regular checkups the doctor was about to send her home when Lucille complained of a severe headache and insisted he re-check her blood pressure. Within sixty minutes she was in an ambulance and 125 km away, being admitted to Foothills Hospital in Calgary. I arranged care for baby David and followed by car. When I arrived at the hospital, Lucille was resting in a darkened room while the doctors were trying to delay what would be a very risky 10 week premature birth. After 10 days of bed rest the Mary was in distress and the doctors decided a Caesarean delivery was necessary. My job was to comfort Lucille on the other side of a small screen. In front of me on the wall was a large sign with a 1 to 10 scale of how to evaluate the health of a newborn baby:

- Strong movement to no movement
- Bright red color to dark purple color
- Weight over 10 lbs to under 2 lbs.
- Strong breathing to not breathing on own

When Mary was briefly shown to Lucille we could see she was on the unhealthy end of all four scales. Mary was immediately put on 98% oxygen. That was the most she could survive. The oxygen caused Bronchial Dysplasia that took years to heal. Mary would not get off oxygen for two years. It was time to pray. We prayed, our friends prayed, and the Cursillo community was invited to pray for Mary. As we all cried out to God for help, I learned to pray from the heart. I learned to love unconditionally. It was a profound experience in spiritual growth.

Lucille and I were both in shock, watching helplessly as this tiny 2 pound 4 oz. miracle lay motionless as machines pumped oxygen into her lungs and food into her stomach. One lung was about 2 inches long and the other smaller. She would have to grow to survive. Surviving the fourth night is critical for premature babies. Mary was losing weight instead of gaining. I knew from studying the Sandfords' books (see below) that we had to pray her personal spirit to life, so it would in turn sustain the life of her body. Lucille had a dream of herself swinging back and forth over a deep gorge. We knew it meant Mary was swinging between life and death.

On the third day we had the first miracle. I "just happened" to meet our priest from Red Deer and Gudrun Schroeder, Mary's godmother, at the elevator going up to Lucille's room. I asked if we could do an emergency baptism. We all put on sterile gowns and masks and went into the Intensive Care Nursery. The priest read the prayer to bless the water. His hand shook as he barely touched Mary's forehead with one drop of water and baptized her in the Name of the Father, the Son and the Holy Spirit. He said later he was afraid to touch her.

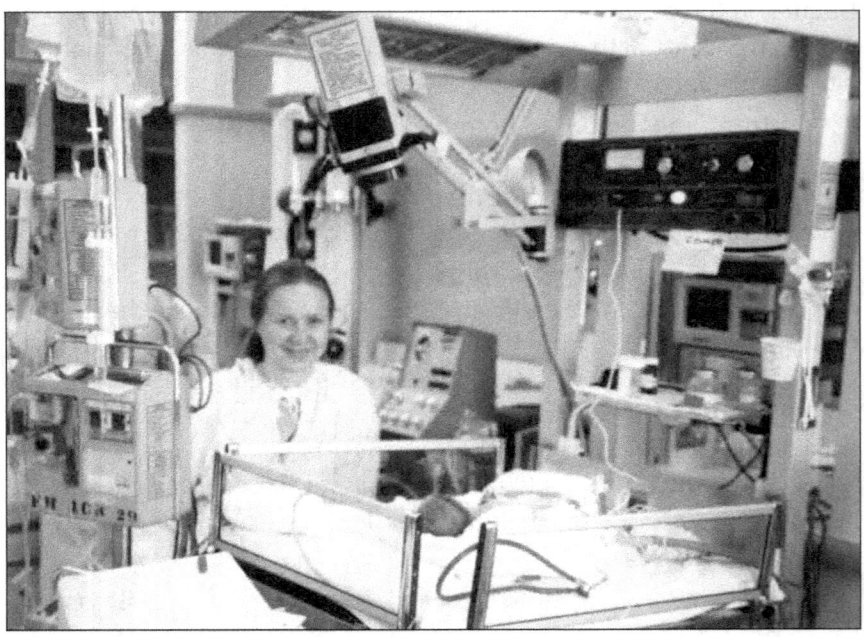

Figure 10.1: Mary and Lucille.

That night a second miracle happened. Gudrun Schroeder was working as team member preparing for a Cursillo Weekend. She told them about Mary and asked the Bishop if they could all pray. He stopped the meeting and called for five minutes of silent prayer for Mary. Across the City in the hospital, we could feel the power. We were filled with joy. Lucille said she felt like dancing so we walked out on a pass for dinner at a nearby restaurant. As the doctors feared the worst I was allowed to sleep over in the hospital room. During the night three different doctors came in to prepare us by saying, "You know Mary is very sick." We knew and kept praying. Lucille went out to Intensive Care early in the morning for some time with Mary. Mary survived! She began to gain weight and after 90 days was strong enough to come off life support and breathe on her own. We could only give thanks to God for our joy.

Mary was in and out of the Children's Hospital and on oxygen for two years. The doctors eventually sent her home with the sobering warning that "If the love of the home does not help her grow, she is on the way to the end." We had an oxygen concentrator that ran constantly with a bump, bump, bump sound that Lucille had to get away from. She would take Mary with a portable oxygen tank and they would lie on a blanket listening to the quiet gurgle of the Red Deer River. Mary was still being fed with a tube into her stomach. This was handy but temporary. It actually popped out once when I was feeding her and I had become so used to medical things I just pushed it back in.

As Mary grew up, we were able to bring her to St. Luke's Church in Red Deer and complete her baptism — with great joy! But life was never easy for Mary. There had been some brain damage from the oxygen and this affected her short-term memory. We had many meetings with psychiatrists, social workers and school counsellors but never completely understood what all the jargon meant. Looking back, it was like dementia. She was intelligent but could not remember things. In Manitoba I taught her the three times table one night and found she had completely forgotten it the next day. This meant that she could not complete a regular school program and could not work at jobs involving remembering orders or making change. Her best job was as a bus girl in a restaurant where the old men loved to talk to her.

What her brain lacked was made up for by her personal spirit. Mary was highly intuitive and could tell instantly if someone was lying. I joked with her that she should be working for the police. She was ahead of us all spiritually and connected with people involved in the healing ministry all around Calgary. One of the reasons I deeply regret leaving St. George's for another interim was that she was thriving there as a member of the healing team. Once when she was on the healing team of a Wholeness Through Christ Workshop in B.C., she witnessed a physical healing miracle. The team of three was surrounded by prayer backup and praying very intensely for a woman who had a headache. Suddenly the woman's leg grew two inches! It had been shorter than the other and was apparently causing the headache.

After Mary completed High School life became more frustrating. She loved her brother David who had played with her and watched over her from the beginning. David was her opposite — gifted in math and economics with perfect body co-ordination, training year-round for Canada's Olympic Cross-Country Ski Team. Mary wanted to live on her own. She moved out for a while but it did not work out and she came home. That same week, a girl she knew at St. Mark's when I was the Interim Priest there, committed suicide. The girl's boyfriend had committed suicide a week earlier and apparently she felt she could not live without him. It was a terrible time, as we sat through the funeral together. Healing ministry is not for sissies — we learned about the ministry of just being present.

Mary went from job to job, finally finding meaning in getting up very early to go downtown and hand out flyers to people getting off the C-Train. Her smile gave them a lift and she was very popular. Her favorite job was looking after two autistic girls. As an extremely intuitive and spiritually alive woman, she could easily understand their needs and care for them. Caring for Mary her taught us to love unconditionally.

Mary was right on the border of self-sufficiency — competent enough to do some kinds of work but not able to remember things. Unfortunately, there were no Social Services programs that could really help her. One of our big mistakes was in letting Social Services take her to a sheltered workshop for people with severe mental challenges. When Mary saw older people who were significantly below her mental level being happy doing simple repetitive work, she became frightened. She probably saw this as own her potential future, and tragically overdosed on Tylenol not long after.

The death was not considered a suicide because she suffered from very painful menstrual cramps and had bought the Tylenol to relieve the pain. She could easily have forgotten how many she had already taken — 17 Tylenol will kill you. Mary was in good spirits on the August long weekend as she and I went downtown for lunch on the Saturday and bought her a laptop. On Sunday morning of the August long weekend Mary was throwing up. Lucille brought her upstairs to our bed and went to the local pharmacy to get some medication. The Pharmacy said there was a bad stomach flu going around and gave us an electrolyte solution for Mary. We knew she would not go to Emergency because of her past experiences. We had to go to the Chinese Anglican Fellowship service that afternoon, followed by a dinner. As Mary settled in our bed she called out, "I love you both." I was in the living room and we both replied, "I love you too." Mary's last words would be "I love you more."

When we came home Mary was sleeping downstairs. The next morning, Lucille who wakes up very early, thought she heard moaning downstairs and went down to check on Mary. Mary was moaning in pain and barely conscious, so we called 911. Within minutes, a fire engine and EMS ambulance arrived. They checked Mary, called the hospital to alert them and a big fireman gently carried her upstairs and out to the ambulance. When Lucille and I got to Emergency, there were already three doctors working on her. The Emergency waiting room was almost empty as it was the Monday of a long weekend. The Chaplain explained that Emergency was empty because "there is no more alcohol left in town." We called David at work and he came. We all prayed with the Chaplain and on our own.

We met with two doctors who talked to us about the possibility of a kidney transplant. We agreed we had to decline as Mary had told us many times she did not want any "heroics" if she went back into hospital. We told the doctors that Mary would not have the memory and self-discipline required to maintain the strict diet and exercise plan required of transplant patients. At lunch time they sent us home while they moved Mary out of the operating room into Intensive Care — six floors below her original Neo-natal Intensive Care room.

We came back to Emergency around 4.30 pm. Mary was still in a coma and not moving. She was hooked up to a dialysis machine that was cleaning her blood to save the kidney. We held her hand, told her we loved her and prayed for another miracle. I called David at work again and told him to come quickly. David arrived and we gathered around the bed. The doctor said "Mary is trying to tell us something." A few minutes later she was gone — as I said later in the Eulogy "surrounded by the love of her family and medical staff just as she had been born." The nurses had done her hair with a pink ribbon. She was beautiful and at peace.

We were in shock for the next year. We were overwhelmed by the kindness of our friends — over 350 came to the funeral. My son Christopher came from Whitehorse and stood up with the family as I read the Eulogy. I was keeping it together fairly well until Lucille's dear friend Jill Burns got up to read the Prayers of the People. She began "I have prayed for Mary Gishler every day of her life, so it is fitting that I should pray for her today." Mary taught us all to pray.

The day after Mary died, I was sitting as usual at the dining room table watching Lucille in the kitchen. Suddenly I could see Mary standing between us. It was like a hologram made of light. She was wearing a white dress with sun and wind blowing her hair. She was smiling. Mary had gone home. Another friend later shared she had also seen a vision of Mary sitting on Jesus' lap. She said Mary seemed to be ministering to Jesus. As we go spiritual, good news always seems to rise up out of bad news.

We may never completely recover from this loss. Lucille and I attended a Grief Support group, which helped us to understand and begin to normalize the situation. They suggested it would take two to four years to reach a "new normal." The first year — and perhaps much of the past seven years, we have been in shock. Lucille and I went on a wonderful trip to Italy, Austria and Hungary shortly after the funeral. The only sign we are still in grief is that Lucille is still not able to pick out a gravestone. Mary is buried in the middle between two huge trees on the Eastern edge of the Riley family plot — with her Great Aunt Louise Riley, librarian and author and Great Grandparents Ezra and Harriet Riley. She taught me to love unconditionally and got us into the healing ministry which has brought us such meaning, purpose and spiritual joy.

10.2 My Slumbering Spirit

My own spiritual wounding started in childhood as described above. I was not wounded physically but emotionally. My father had a very demanding position, and had suffered as a "preachers kid" from emotional neglect by his father. He was not able to have an emotional relationship with me. My mother had also been traumatized by the death of her mother at age 12, and the loss of her eldest brother in WWI. I was well cared for materially, but was an emotionally abandoned child (with a dog who loved me). Many years later I discovered the connection between emotional abandonment and a slumbering spirit in the writings of John and Paula Sandford. Lucille and I studied *The Transformation of the Inner Man* (1982) and *Healing the Wounded Spirit* (1985) when we were in Red Deer. Our little study group also listened to tapes of their talks at healing workshops. Much later, after we came back to Calgary in 1995, we met John and Paula at one of their healing workshops in Okotoks, just south of Calgary. It was a wonderful experience to hug the man I had long regarded as my primary mentor in inner healing. I discovered that my spiritual healing began when I began to experience the warm physical affection of Lucille. Like everyone else, I needed to be loved to develop a spiritual life.

One of their major contributions to the body of knowledge on healing is their teaching on the Slumbering Spirit.[48] This helped me understand why some people are spiritually aware, and others are not. Some people are able to see and understand how things work in the spiritual dimension while others seem blind or deaf. The Apostle Paul writes that for some reason "…God gave them a spirit of stupor, eyes that see not and ears to hear not, down to this very day." (Romans 11.8).

Discovering the concept of a slumbering spirit was not easy. The Sandfords had ministered to a number of Spirit-filled evangelists, clergy and lay people, who were getting into seriously sinful situations like adultery. These people could preach good, evangelical sermons; then go out and commit the same sins they had just preached against. They did not seem to have a functioning conscience. John was particularly disgusted and disturbed by one traveling evangelist with a successful healing ministry who committed adultery, got a young woman pregnant, pressured her into having an abortion, then denied he had ever known her. Like me, he finally prayed that most theologically sophisticated prayer, "Help"! Like the prophets of old he got a clear message from God:

> "John, these people do not have an alert and functioning spirit. Their own personal spirit is not awake. They have a slumbering spirit."[49]

He went on to discover that the root cause was that their personal spirit was alive at birth but had never been "...met, loved and nurtured through warm physical affection."[50] Their spirit had either fallen asleep in infancy, or later on when they had failed to establish a warm love relationship with God or others through worship, prayer and warm physical affection. The result was a hardening of their heart, like a wall around their spirit, that separated them from God and other people emotionally and spiritually. They could do and say all the right things, but had only head knowledge of God and other people. In addition to not having a functioning conscience to warn them about spiritually destructive behaviour, they could not fully enjoy the benefits of spiritual relationships:
- Not experiencing God's love during prayer time and public worship
- Not hearing the voice of God
- No Intuitive, creative and emotional thinking and communicating

- Minus the joy in committed marital sexual relations

Watchman Nee calls these people "soulish" because they are living out of their soul (where the mind is), as opposed to living by their personal spirit.[51] This is a very common spiritual wound in both evangelical and liberal Christian churches. It helps us understand the gulf between what we might describe as spiritual people and religious people. The current bitter dispute over blessing and marrying same-sex couples in some churches, may be an example of Christians dividing into spiritual and religious camps with opposing perspectives (and or self-deception). Sadly this wound can be spiritually fatal.

> "Many will say to me on that day, 'Lord, lord did we not prophecy in your name, and in your name cast out demons, and in your name perform many miracles?' And I will declare to them, I never knew you. Depart from me, you who practice lawlessness." (Matt. 7.22-23)

My heart is broken because, like many others, my slumbering spirit was lost in the strongholds of intellectualism and liberalism. I have gone from being raised in a liberal and intellectual family to reading the Bible, and becoming an annoying and overly judgemental evangelical to experiencing real love, the Holy Spirit, supernatural healing and becoming a balanced spiritual person. My personal spirit began to come alive through the incredible love of Lucille. This is the something more she gave me, in addition to Catherine Marshall's book. This has confirmed for me what the Sandfords teach about healing a slumbering spirit.

10.3 Sexual Abuse

Sexual abuse[52] is the most common and widespread form of emotional and spiritual wounding. We have been amazed at the number of abused women who came to us for help. Fortunately, by this time we were more mature and better prepared through the teaching of the Sandfords', Family Foundations International and Wholeness through Christ.

The Sandfords were pioneers in this now tragically common healing issue. Their very simple practice of spiritual discernment, in working back from "the fruit" to "the spiritual root," helped me understand how prayer ministry works. Sexual abuse seems rampant in our post-Christendom and post- truth culture. Many people have now become so self-centred and narcissistic, that they have lost their fear of God and their hope of eternal spiritual life. The result is high-stress and fear-based lives, that easily get into re-creational sex and sexual abuse. I discovered the deception of sex as false love while writing my unpublished *Seven Great Deceptions* manuscript in 1986.

The Sandfords had suggested three steps in healing sexual abuse which we generally tried to follow, along with what we learned at other workshops.[53] Our ministry to sexually abused women generally began by listening to the emotional pain of the abused woman. We needed to get from the fruit to the root by understanding their family background and relationship with the abuser. The Sandfords taught us to begin ministry by trying to change the attitude of the abused person from judgement and hatred of the abuser to understanding and compassion. Research has shown that most abusers have been abused themselves as children. They are usually deeply wounded by their own anger at an abuser. Next, we explained the Sandfords' spiritual law of Sowing and Reaping. This explains how people who sow anger and judgement in their lives, are bound to that anger and end up reaping even more anger and judgement. This bounces back like a ball hitting a wall and getting bigger when it comes back at them. Un-forgiveness is the most common and destructive sin we have dealt with. The good news in all this is that real forgiveness from the heart is possible through a very specific repentance, confession and absolution process.

The other side of this is, as the Lord's Prayer requires, that if we sow forgiveness in our lives, we reap forgiveness. We also explained to these women how legalistic things are in the spiritual dimension. Even though they had every right to be angry and hate the abuser, anger is still a sin that may have continuing spiritual power over them, if not repented and confessed and taken to the Cross for forgiveness.

Prayer ministry generally began with a time of inviting the Holy Spirit to come and guide and protect us. The Sandfords' recommended first step in ministry is to purify ourselves and create a holy environment by all repenting and confessing our part in an abusive culture, that accepts pornography. Our culture has reduced sexual activity from holy and sacred communion in marriage, to a mechanical act of objectified false pleasure.

The next step was to lead the wounded person through a process of repentance and confession, to forgiveness and healing. This was based on the spiritual roots we had discovered in counselling. This forgiveness and healing ministry is sometimes counter-intuitive. For example, we naturally feel we should be comforting rather than challenging the angry and abused person. The problem is that in the spiritual dimension, things are much more legalistic than human wisdom assumes. For example, the victim could not help but feel helplessness, anger, rage and frustration at the abuser.

While these judgements are perfectly natural and expected in our human thinking, they are like spiritual boat anchors, tying the victim to the situation and the abuser. The victim's feelings of anger, hate and rage are like an energy field, a tractor beam for older *Star Trek* fans. These sinful reactions will not lose their power of guilt and shame until they are repented, confessed and taken to the Cross for forgiveness and healing. We have discovered that unforgiveness is a common and powerful sin that can paralyze a person spiritually. When we forgive, often by asking the Holy Spirit to give us the grace to forgive (because we cannot do this on our own), we feel tremendous freedom and peace. Anger, for example, is nothing less than murder in the heart. It is almost as serious as actual murder, because we have failed to love and it is our deliberate intent to kill. This intent is the legal difference between manslaughter (accidental killing) and (pre-meditated) murder.

From our experience with Family Foundations International we were able to go back in prayer and visioning with the victims, and all see the abuse. We were able to invite Jesus to come into the situation and stand with us. We all repented and confessed our guilt of living in a culture of pornography. We asked Jesus to forgive us, and heard and accepted His words of forgiveness. Next, we asked the victim if she could forgive the abuser, or at least speak her intent, by asking the Holy Spirit to give her the strength to forgive the abuser. The women were also able to ask Jesus to forgive the abuser. This demonstrated their complete letting go of the trauma, as a follow-up step in healing.

The work of reconciliation and healing prayer often includes confessing the sin of believing a lie. This is also counter-intuitive, but this is how things work in the legalistic supernatural dimension. For example a woman may have believed she was partly responsible for the abuse through her own provocative dress or actions. At the very least, she would need to be reassured that this is a common lie from the evil one. This lie is a denial of God's Word, that God's creation of men and women is "very good." If she had believed this lie, we led her through the repentance, confession and accepting forgiveness process; to break the sin-guilt and free her from the destructive power of the lie.

We ended the ministry by sealing any wounds, which can be demonic spiritual doorways; with the shed blood of Jesus. We also spent a long time soaking these women in the healing balm of the Holy Spirit and assuring them of God's love and Jesus forgiveness. Women should also be given a "Father's Blessing." I would ask permission to act in the place of their father, and pronounce this blessing over them. This is an ancient Jewish custom of a father telling a precious daughter that she is now ready to leave the father's protection and go out in the world as a beautiful, gifted woman. She is also ready to come under the protection of a husband, and have her own family, or to follow the desires of her heart. Fathers need to audibly tell daughters that they are clever, intelligent and perfect in the eyes of God.

These ministry sessions generally lasted an hour or more and were very intense. We often just sat with the person in silence, as the mind caught up to the new feelings of freedom and peace. We suggested they be very good to themselves for the next week, as they adjusted to these new feelings and not be too busy for prayer, Bible reading and listening to the Holy Spirit. As many were un-churched we also tried to connect them to a church community where they could receive further teaching and warm loving fellowship. In spite of the trauma, it was wonderful to see the grace of Jesus take away their guilt and shame — freeing them from a terrible spiritual burden. Our reward was seeing the joy on the faces of these women as they left.

10.4 The Spirit of Cancer

Cancer has become the great fear of our time. Almost everyone my age has either had cancer or seen a close friend or relative go through the often long and debilitating process of dying from cancer. My mother was an early cancer survivor in spite of being a serious smoker. Her sister, the Canadian author and librarian Louse Riley, died of cancer in our house when I was a teenager. She was my favourite aunt and dedicated her first book *The Mystery Horse* to me. I followed in her footsteps as a President of the Library Association of Alberta. Aunt Louise loved children, and I began wondering if her sadness at never marrying contributed to the cancer. While I have no medical training, I have observed that many of the people I know who have died of cancer had tragic life histories. My logical mind has wondered for a long time if cancer, which as I understand it is something going wrong with the body's immune cells, is the fruit of a deep root of hurt and sadness. I wonder if sadness or discouragement in life can wound the personal spirit to the point of physical death through immune deficiency.

My first experience in praying for the healing of cancer came at a Camps Farthest Out Healing Workshop at Gull Lake, Alberta, around 1996. The speaker was an Anglican priest and member of the Order of St. Luke, from Washington State. He was truly anointed in the healing ministry. After three days of worship, teaching and prayer, there was a powerful healing service. We were in deep prayer for a woman suffering from cancer. The priest took authority over the spirit of cancer, and we could all see a black mass like a dark cloud being pulled upwards from the woman's head. We could also see blue (the color of healing) flames on the priest's fingertips, as he gently drew the Spirit out and sent it directly to Jesus, to go where Jesus commanded. Later we all got involved in praying for each other. I was astonished to see the same blue flames coming out of my own fingertips as I prayed over people. This confirmed my suspicion that there is a demon or evil spirit of cancer, and taught me how to pray for cancer patients.

Since then there have been no more blue flames, and two of the three people we have prayed for since have died. This ministry should probably be done by more experienced people, and surrounded by more intense prayer support than we have had so far. The good news is that the two people who died did live an extra year beyond what their doctors expected. The great tragedy is that thousands more could be helped, if more Christian churches really believed in and encouraged the development of serious prayer ministry. Prayer ministry cannot always heal cancer, but it can always cleanse and strengthen the personal spirit in the fight against cancer. Patients will always need medical care to repair the biological damage that has been done.

Chapter 11

Wounds from Personal or Inherited Sin-Guilt

There is a very relevant joke about sin. The wife comes home from church. The husband greets her and asks her what the sermon was about. "He talked about sin," she said. "What did he say about sin?" he asked. "He was against it," she said. The point is that the teaching on sin in many churches is shallow and superficial. Many Christians do not understand, in depth and detail, how things work in the supernatural dimension and why sin is so destructive. They are not taught how sin works in the spiritual dimension to damage and destroy our personal spiritual life, and how these spiritual wounds affect our daily lives. In this chapter, I am sharing the practical details of how my own sin and inherited sin affected my life and how I have been healed.

11.1 The Law of Sowing and Reaping

> "Do not be deceived: God cannot be mocked. A man reaps what he sows." (Galatians 6.7)[54]

We have already seen how the law of sowing and reaping had bound sexual abuse victims to their abusers through the destructive power of un-forgiveness. Even though the abused women would seem to have every right to be angry at the abuser, the bottom line was that she had murder in her heart. That natural response of anger sowed sin-guilt in her heart, that bounced back with multiplied power as she reaped a harvest of even greater anger. Anger bound her spiritually to the trauma for years.

The thing about spiritual laws is that they are immutable: not flexible, not bendable and not avoidable. Even God will not just forgive us if we go on with our own selfish or soulish life.[55] This is where theological liberals may go dangerously wrong in assuming God is limited to our human idea of love, and must automatically forgive us because he loves us. This is a heretical lie that denies the need for Jesus death for the sins of the whole world. The Sandfords point out that God created a physical world that operates on discoverable physical laws like the law of gravity. I have often quoted their example of the dead person who did not believe in the law of Gravity and stepped off a high roof. God also created the spiritual dimension according to spiritual laws: sin leads to spiritual death. It doesn't matter if you are a child, a fool or a very nice person. If you do the crime, you do the time. This is where the good news of Jesus is so important. God has given us complete freedom and cannot get around or suspend the law of sin leading to death in His revealed Word. He can and has created a new spiritual law, that accepts that real repentance (dying emotionally to a sin), and verbally asking Jesus in faith to forgive us; is acceptable as the required death. What must die inside us is our specific rebellion against God. This helps us overcome our self-centred nature and its control of our soul as in Chapter 2 on page 9.

By understanding the law of sowing and reaping, we come to the most helpful idea from the Sandfords' regarding healing ministry. "If you've got the fruit, you've got the root." The key to prayer ministry is to ask a lot of questions and follow the presenting problem back in time to a childhood, family or relationship root. In my case the fruit was my reaction to criticism. My father was a brilliant scientist, managing a large research staff. He taught me to criticise current events, politicians and just about any idea that did not seem right to him. This is how our family avoided talking about personal issues. Nobody believes me when I tell them my parents were completely stunned when I told them who I was about to marry. There is a saying that a child raised on criticism will grow up to be a critic. That would be me. My growing up during the cold war, under the threat of imminent nuclear incineration, was a powerful motivation for analysis and criticism. The problem is, criticism can become a sin. Criticism of another person is often unloving, judgemental, unforgiving, arrogant and a contradiction of God's statement in Genesis that creation was "very good."

> "But I tell **you** that anyone who is angry with a brother or sister will be subject to judgment. Again, anyone who **says** to a brother or sister, 'Raca,' is answerable to the court. And anyone who **says, 'You fool!'** will be in danger of the fire of hell." (Matthew 5.22 NIV)

Words spoken have power. Words are powerful as blessings or curses. Careful reading of the Creation story in Genesis reveals that each stage of creation began when "God said let there be...." When I say "you fool" or some other criticism, something happens in the supernatural dimension. The other person does not instantly become a complete fool, but something is triggered in the supernatural. Perhaps I am empowering or giving rights to destructive spirits, to gradually blind that person to some wisdom. It works, but I have no idea how it works, except that I am guilty of the sin of placing a curse on someone. That is witchcraft and forbidden. "The acts of the flesh are obvious: sexual immorality, debauchery, idolatry and witchcraft...I warn you, as I did before, that those who live like this will not inherit the kingdom of God." (Galatians 5.19-21)

My spiritual life has often been polluted and wounded by my out-of-order criticisms. It would have been nice if I could have just repented of this once, and been completely healed. The problem is my human weakness and fallibility which means I often fail to learn from mistakes, fall back into judgement and need further forgiveness and healing.

Another example of personal sin leading to wounding is what the Sandfords call "bitter root judgements." Bitter-root judgements are a practical application of the Law of Sowing and Reaping at work in our spirit and soul.[56] This concept helped me greatly in ministry, and is also developed in *Healing the Wounded Spirit*.[57] The Bible warns us not to judge other people:

> "See to it that no one comes short of the grace of God, that no root of bitterness springing up causes trouble, and by it may be defiled." (Heb. 12.5)
>
> "Do not judge lest you be judged yourselves. For in the way you judge, you will be judged, and by your standard of measure, it will be measured to you." (Matt. 7.1-2)

Like many of the people we have prayed for, I had of course dishonoured my father by judging him as unloving, judgemental and uncaring about my emotional life. There is an embarrassing story of my noticing the pictures on the shelves of our den. Front and centre were pictures of us, our children, Lucille's sister — and my beloved dog Robbie. No pictures of my or Lucille's parents. Lucille observed that Robbie was the one who gave me the love my parents failed to give. From a worldly point of view this was justice and there was nothing wrong. Then there is spiritual rule number 5 — the Fifth Commandment:

> "Honor your father and your mother, so that you may live long in the land the Lord your God is giving you."

Notice it does not say you have to like your parents or agree with them. It says you have to honour them: treat them with the respect their place deserves. They are the ones who gave you life and from whom you will pass on a family history to the next generation. In Hebrew tradition, the mother and father acted as representatives of God on Earth, in passing on spiritual wisdom to their children. This special task of parents has been tragically lost in Western culture, and at great cost to the current generation. I was able to go through the repentance, confession and absolution process to be forgiven and freed from this sin-guilt and bondage.

11.2 "Shrikeism" and Listening to the Holy Spirit

Christian counsellors and those in healing ministry have an enormous advantage over psychological analysis. They can pray for and receive critical help from the Holy Spirit. I learned this when Lucille and I were attending Beth Shechinah, a Messianic Jewish congregation. I was in spiritual turmoil from the strife over same-sex blessings in the Anglican Church and needed a time out. A woman attending Beth Shechinah invited us to come to her house and pray for her continuing problems in relationship with men. She had asked us to take her through the breaking of Masonic oaths and curses prayers, which had changed our own lives. We were also assuming (wrongly) that she had probably also been abused. In response to a nudge from the Holy Spirit for me to be a little humble and ask for help, I prayed and got the word "shrike."

A shrike is a particularly vicious and cruel bird. It that impales its victim alive on a thorn bush, and then tears it apart. I remembered that the Sandfords had defined shrikism, as a particular pattern of destructive behaviour that comes out of performance orientation. Shrikism is more common in women, who are naturally more wired to nurture and please. If they have learned from experience that being perfect, or holy and righteous saints earns them love and attention, they may try to suck all the holiness and righteousness out of a relationship. This leaves nothing for their spouse. In fact the spouse finds he gets more attention by being the unholy one, the failure who makes the shrike look good. She can then pick apart all his faults publically and bask in the glory and attention of holy martyrdom.

When we arrived at the house and shared this, the woman broke down, confessed and we were able to lead her to repentance, confession and freedom from the lie that Jesus would not love her unless she was perfect. This broke the power of her spiritual guilt and freed her to have a real love relationship with Jesus.

11.3 Generational Sin:
Healing the Family Tree

I have learned that sin-guilt can be passed down several generations and be the root cause of wounds that affect people's lives from both the Bible and personal experience. In 2001, we attended a Wholeness Through Christ workshop at the Entheos retreat centre just West of Calgary. Wholeness is a very informal association of mostly lay people in Canada and the U.S. They gather in different cities, at their own expense, to put on four-day healing workshops. Ours started with lots of singing, praise music and a brief presentation of their healing model (as above) "... Yet He does not leave the **guilty** unpunished; He punishes the children and their children for the **sin** of the parents to the third and fourth **generation**." (Exodus 34.7 NIV).

What was most striking about my Wholeness ministry was the inherited sin-guilt from my parents. I was stunned to find out I had a Viking root of sin! The Vikings had travelled to what is now northern Germany, and murdered, raped and pillaged their way along the coast. Imagine how the survivors felt. They would have been overwhelmed by tremendous anger, rage and grief. They would have spoken terrible curses of death and destruction on their enemies. These curses had real power over both the Vikings (and their soon to be born offspring left behind), and on the people who spoke them. Curses bounce back. Fast forward several hundred years, and my grandfather is born in Frielingen, northern Germany. This same grandfather, a godly Evangelical United Brethren pastor, had apparently passed this Viking sin-guilt on through my father. The consequence was, I had to stand in the gap for all of my ancestors, including the Vikings, and repent, confess and receive forgiveness from Jesus for what they had done. I also had to repent, confess and ask forgiveness for my German roots; and the sins of pride, lack of love, military sprit (gunfighter), perfectionism, intellectualism, regimentation and cold love. I also had to forgive my ancestors for passing this sin-guilt on, and place the Cross between me and my children and our ancestors. This broke the power of the sin-guilt that was oppressing me, and released me from bondage.

From my mother, they discerned that I had also inherited the sinful English roots of pride, arrogance, deception and rage. The team led me meticulously through the repentance, confession and absolution process for each root of sin, and healed the relationship with both my mother and father. I also had to repent, confess and receive forgiveness for believing a lie from a counsellor, that because I had not developed political skills as a youth, I could never develop them.

Human characteristics seem to be inheritable and the Sandfords share ways in which their children exhibited some unusual characteristics of their parents. Their point is that "... we may inherit our propensity to sin through our genes."[58]

The best example of generational sin is a story that I have often heard at healing conferences about the Jukes and Adams families. Very briefly, the history of the Jukes and Adams families in the United States illustrates both inherited characteristics and learning by example. The Jukes ancestors were an atheist couple who had about 16 descendents in three generations. Several were hung for murder, most of the men spent time in jail and all of the families were on welfare at some time. In contrast, the Adams family began with a Christian couple, whose descendents in three generations included a President, Vice-President of the United States, a university president, several judges and many lawyers and company presidents. None of their descendents was ever in jail or on welfare.

The classic book on healing generational sin is *Healing the Family Tree* by Kenneth McAll. McAll was a medical doctor in China during the Japanese/Chinese civil war. He was the son of missionaries and became interested in the Chinese belief in evil spirits. On one of his treks to a remote hospital clinic, he met a man dressed entirely in white, who directed him to a nearby village, saying there were many wounded people there who needed him.[59] The man vanished as he entered the village gate. The villagers told McAll that the village he was originally heading for had been captured by the Japanese, and that he had been headed into an ambush. He realized the man who had saved him was Jesus.

Later, back in the U.K., McAll studied psychiatry and worked in mental hospitals. He discovered that he could help some people who did not respond to psychiatric treatment by praying for them. After in-depth interviews he discovered that these "hard cases" often had ancestors who had not been given a Christian burial, or had been involved in occult practices. He worked with Anglican clergy, to celebrate a special Eucharist with prayers for healing the family tree. This was very successful in healing these people and freeing them from the spiritual wounds of inherited sin-guilt. He also had visions of some of their ancestors being dramatically healed, after being restored to a right relationship with Jesus.

With this as background information, I was able to include brief healing prayers for Lucille's family line in one of our Sunday Eucharist services at Sundre. McAll teaches that the historic Holy Communion service has special power for healing, as the prayers connect people spiritually to the sacrificial death of Jesus and the power of the Cross in healing sin-guilt. We drew up a Paulson Family tree which was placed on the altar. Her parents served in China as missionaries. We had been told that half of the missionaries who came back from China had picked up demonic spirits. Christians can be demonized (in spite of what some churches teach).

I said the prayer of consecration and prayed healing over the whole family line to include any who may not have died in a state of peace with God. Then I placed the Cross of Jesus in prayer between past and present generations, to prevent their sin-guilt from continuing down the line and polluting later generations. Finally, I prayed the shed blood of Jesus up and down the generational line to cleanse and seal it. Lucille and I both had a wonderful sense of peace after this service.

Chapter 12

Delivering Prisoners:
Spiritual Oppression, Bondage and Strongholds

The really bad news is that un-forgiven sin, like a baby dragon, does not just eventually go away. It grows and gains in strength and destructive power. Just as in psychology, where bad choices can lead to bad habits and destructive behaviour; in the spiritual dimension, wounds can lead to spiritual oppression and bondage. Sin, like all bad choices, can be a slippery slope to destruction. In this section we will share examples of freeing people from the oppression and bondage of sexual sin, alcoholism, Masonic oaths and curses, identity theft, homosexuality and depression. Spiritual wounds open doorways for the demonic to live inside a person and oppress them more effectively. Just as the damage of sin gets more dangerous, the ministry of healing prayer becomes more dangerous, and needs to be done by more experienced people and surrounded with more prayer support. At this point we have moved from healing spiritual wounds to restore people to right-relationship with Jesus, to healing spiritual wounds to free people from the captivity or bondage of evil spirits. This change of focus is called deliverance ministry (as in deliver us from evil) or exorcism. Many people are frightened by the demonic but this is a central part of the healing ministry of Jesus. Going back to Jesus' mission statement we notice there is deeper

and deeper healing as:
1. The Good News of healing is proclaimed so that
2. Freedom is proclaimed to the prisoners (to false teachings) so that
3. The blind have their (spiritual) eyes opened so that
4. The (spiritually) oppressed are freed (delivered)

One of the keys to understanding biblical passages is that the psalms for example are written from the general (God loves his people) to the more specific (God rescues them). This is Jesus teaching technique in explaining His (our) healing ministry.

12.1 Sexual Bondage and Alcoholism

Most people know that alcoholism is a serious condition that is extremely difficult to treat because it generally includes both psychological issues and a biological/chemical addiction. What is interesting is that the program with the best success rate is the 12 Step program of Alcoholics Anonymous. The Fifth Step of this program includes a whole life self examination, and written confession of sin taken to a priest for absolution. Before sharing my experience in freeing a man from the bondage of alcoholism let me explain how the sin of drinking/eating/wanting anything in excess can lead first to spiritual oppression and then to spiritual bondage.

I use the example of alcoholism to explain spiritual oppression and bondage, as alcoholism is the most common and visible example both of spiritual oppression and spiritual bondage. As in the diagram above, when someone rebels against God's order by polluting his body with too much alcohol (or food or drugs etc.), he is guilty of sin. This sin can cause a spiritual wound if it is repeated and becomes a habit. Spiritual wounds can act as doorways for evil spirits to enter a person and oppress them from inside. Spiritual oppression from the inside is more powerful. Imagine an uninvited voice in your head constantly urging destructive behaviour. This is where outside temptation becomes internal oppression of the mind and soul. This intensifies the battle for control of the will as described in Chapter 2. If the pattern of drinking excessively continues, this spiritual oppression may grow stronger until the temptation to have another drink becomes overwhelming, and the person is powerless to say no. At this point we can say someone is in spiritual bondage to a spirit of alcoholism.

The act of intimate physical sexual touch connects our spirits to the spirit of the one we touch. Here I can testify to my own healing experience. Before my marriage to Lucille, I had been on a retreat, conducted a self-examination and gone to a Roman Catholic priest for confession. He taught me the importance of severing the spiritual link to my ex-wife, which could lead to spiritual pollution continuing to flow between us, and affect my relationship with Lucille. He included a prayer of severing in the words of absolution after my confession. This freed me to have a wonderful spiritual relationship with Lucille, free of past baggage. I recommend this to all couples as part of marriage preparation.

The Sandfords had helped me understand the spiritual reason behind the biblical ban on sexual relationships outside a marriage relationship: the "why," behind the "don't": "And don't you know that if a man joins himself to a prostitute, she becomes part of him and he becomes part of her. For God tells us that in His sight the two become one person" (1 Cor. 6.16, 17).

Years later a man came to see me for the confession required as part of a 12 step alcoholism program. He had written out a whole life confession — a serious pile of paper that boiled down to unmarried sexual relationships with about twenty women. The problem is that they were still "spiritually married" as a consequence of the sexual relationship. As the Sandfords taught me, all his spiritual pollution had flowed into each of them, and the spiritual pollution of the 20 women had flowed back into his spirit. No wonder he thought he needed a drink!

Following the Sandfords' teaching, we went to prayer and invited the Holy Spirit to come and give us both a vision of him in a field with all 20 women standing around him in a large circle. We could both see the silver cord joining silver spiritual cords (the pipeline) joining his spirit to their spirits. He went around the circle, recognized most of them, and asked them each to forgive him. He repented, asked Jesus to forgive him and accepted forgiveness. I was able to take authority in the name of Jesus and send all his spiritual garbage back to him and the woman's garbage back to them. Next, I asked the Holy Spirit to give me a spiritual sword, and allow me to take authority to go around the circle, severing all the connections. We could both see this in a vision. I then prayed for the cleansing and sealing of the spirits of each woman and the man, with the shed blood of Jesus, and gave thanks for the healing. The man's feet were above the floor as he left; he was now free of the guilt and shame that were at least contributing to, if not driving his alcoholism.

12.2 Homosexuality/Gender Confusion

I have been wrestling with the very sensitive and explosive issue of how the Christian church should relate to people who are sexually attracted to others of the same sex for over 25 years. As noted above, this issue is the push behind the liberal theological deconstruction of historic Christianity. The (false) killer argument of the gay and lesbian community has been that if God created them this way, the church cannot judge their behaviour as sinful (in spite of biblical condemnation). They have argued successfully that Jesus commanded us to love one another and we must accept and love them as equals. I briefly accepted this argument and was comfortable with same-sex blessing. Same-sex marriage however, was a bar I could not jump over, as marriage is a sacrament in the Anglican Church. It is a holy covenant and incompatible with unholy sexual practices.

What jarred me out of even considering same-sex marriage as a holy sacrament was discovering that men and women can be healed from sexual identity confusion. I heard two men and a women at a conference share how they had been deeply into same-sex relationships and then healed through prayer ministry. The woman is now happily married to a (male) Anglican priest. The killer argument against the Church blessing same-sex marriages should have been the clear biblical teaching that it was sinful. But current liberal theology has so de-constructed the authority of the Bible that we seem to need a new killer argument. That argument is that sexual identity confusion can be healed through prayer ministry. Healing through prayer proves that sexual confusion is not normal, healthy or "how made God me." It is a genetic accident or the consequence of the development of a mental stronghold as described above. It is shameful that the leadership in the Anglican Church has consistently refused to let these healed individuals speak, or have a real voice in the public same-sex marriage "dialogue." I have had two articles on this topic rejected for publication by the *Anglican Journal*.

We have described above how mental strongholds are built into a developing character or identity through a combination of mental self-deception and demonic delusion. John and Paula Sandford broke new ground in describing their experiences in healing homosexuals and others with sexual identity confusion in *Transformation of the Inner Man* in 1982. Their explanation of how Satan works to destroy God's creation through sexual identity confusion has helped us in many healing ministry experiences. His bringing together of Jung's psychological concept of archetypes with the Biblical description of Principalities and Strongholds is a significant contribution to human knowledge.[60]

> The weapons we fight with are not the weapons of the world. On the contrary, they have divine power to demolish strongholds. We demolish arguments and every pretension that sets itself up against the knowledge of God, and we take captive every thought to make it obedient to Christ. (2 Corinthians 4-5).

Jung developed the concept of archetypes to explain how thoughts and memories in the unconscious mind seem to be organized into patterns or clusters — i.e., lying, cheating, deceiving, confusing all together. Sandford redefines these archetypes as destructive patterns of thinking and feeling and calls them mental strongholds. He developed the idea that the evil spirits or demons that attack us from the outside, are also organized by these same patterns and controlled by a more powerful demon or principality. This is enormously helpful in ministering to people with a confused sexual identity. "In the case of homosexuals the archetype always has the principality of delusion behind it."[61] This helps us understand why argument and debate is so futile and frustrating in trying to find a compromise on same-sex marriage. Sandford wisely suggests believing Christians must be perfectly clear that people (including clergy) with a confused sexual identity, who refuse to seek healing, must neither be persecuted by Christians or allowed to hold places of leadership in churches.[62]

"Fear is the primary weapon of strongholds. We fear letting go and trusting in the goodness of God."[63] This fear prevents the person from really hearing the truth through the process of self-deception as described above. Healing may involve ongoing ministry to ensure the truth is getting through. Since the Bible teaches us that perfect love casts out fear (1 John 4.18), healing ministry must include a great deal of love by both the counsellor and a supportive church community. This love can overcome the defensive lies and delusions that are preventing the stronghold from hearing the truth. Sandford also suggests silently binding the strong man to keep the ministry focussed on speaking truth to the delusions and lies of the stronghold.

Sandford affirms that we are all naturally created with both a male and a female side. Usually the stronger side matches the biological body sex. But sometimes it does not. As that these missmatches can be inherited, the first part of ministry is to trace back to the root, and identify any root of sin as described above. Nurture may also lead to a personal decision to abandon one sexual side for the other as a result of traumatic experiences with parents or other childhood authority figures: camp counsellors, teachers, priests, etc. Inner vows against parents can bounce back to upset the natural sexual identity balance. Sandford notes that "In all our years of counselling, we have never found a homosexual or a lesbian who had or related well to a strong, gentle loving father."[64]

He shares a dramatic vision he had in healing ministry for a man under the stronghold of homosexuality. After the counselling and preliminary ministry as recommended above, Sandford went to prayer for guidance by the Holy Spirit. He was guided by a vision and prophetic instructions, to see the crossed sexual poles inside the man, and later watch as the hand of God reached inside the man and un-crossing the sexual poles:

> "John, when you have done all this for a homosexual, by vision see the poles reversed as I have shown you, and stand aside and see as I reach in to disentangle those poles and set them in order."[65]

Ten years later Sandford received a letter from this man thanking him for this ministry which had changed his life and completely, and freed him from the stronghold of homosexuality.[66] Since this story was published in 1982 over 240,000 copies of *Transformation of the Inner Man* have been sold. It is unfortunate that since then many churches have chosen to ignore these teachings, affirm homosexuality as normal and imprison people, rather than offering healing and deliverance ministry and freeing them for a life of Christian joy. Homosexuality has now become a destructive corporate stronghold in these churches and in modern secular culture.

12.3 Masonic Oaths and Curses

The Sandfords' teaching helped me in dealing with Masonic oaths and curses.[67] During my Interim ministry in central Alberta I was working with Anglican Churches that were in steep decline. They were generally discouraged as the young people had almost all gone. It was hard to get anyone interested in developing a strategic plan for parish growth. An Anglican priest had been driven out of one, ostensibly because he had offended just about everyone. While he did have an above average ability to offend people, the real reason turned out to be his sacrificial love and courage in exposing the Masons on the Parish Council, as belonging to an occult society. He explained to me that the real reason the Anglican Churches were not growing was that many of these towns had a Masonic Lodge. There was a rival (satanic) church in town.

On the surface the Masons are a wonderful benevolent society for families and children. If a mason loses his job or dies, his brother Masons will help him or the family recover. They are those cute old men called Shriner's that ride funny carts in parades to raise money for children's hospitals. It looks good on the surface, but there is a darker side. We got to know a woman whose father had been a top official, the Worshipful Master. Notice the heresy and idolatry in the title. The First Commandment is to love God and worship Him only. Masons honour the Great Architect (who is really Satan to them) and mock Jesus resurrection. Like the Alchemists, Gnostics, Pelagians and Humanists before them, the Masons promise to lead brothers to a higher understanding of God. This wisdom is learned in degrees, as new brothers are initiated into ever higher levels of understanding. There are generally 33 degrees, depending on which rite is followed.

Each degree includes ceremonies with oaths and curses to ensure the secrecy of the teachings. These oaths, taken over several years, mock and basically de-program Christianity. They are very emotionally powerful and spiritually traumatizing.The men take off their wedding ring and wear a Masonic ring at meetings to prove their real loyalty. The oaths and curses they put on themselves and their descendents if they ever reveal Masonic secrets include being disembowelled, hung and buried within a cable length (6 feet) of the ocean. It reminded me of a news story about a famous banker found mysteriously hanging under London Bridge (with his feet near tidewater). These oaths and curses are witchcraft, contrary to the Bible, a rebellion against God's authority and sinful. They result in sin-guilt and spiritual wounds that can open doorways for demons and be passed down the generational line.

Lucille and I met a woman in Calgary who had a prayer ministry of delivering people from these oaths and curses. She asked us if anyone in either of our families had ever been involved with the Masons. Lucille remembered that her grandfather was a Mason. Since things did not seem to be going well for us at the time, we agreed to go through a three hour renunciation workshop. We were given a 14 page guide to follow. We went through all 33 Masonic degrees in various rites and renounced, repented and confessed each oath our ancestors may have taken. We asked Jesus to forgive us in proxy for our ancestor, and cancel its power of sin-guilt. We felt freed from something that was holding us back in our marriage and in having prosperity. We were told it was a spirit of poverty and lack. This led to us offering the same healing workshop to several other people. There are at least two versions of these Masonic vow renunciations available on the internet and more information under Healing Ministry on my blog www.spirituallifeteaching.info.

12.4 Identity Theft and Low Self-esteem

Our experience is that women who are abused often have low self-esteem. We were amazed at how common this is and how easy it is to free them from the spiritual bondage of believing a lie about themselves. We had learned how to pray for this healing ministry through Family Foundations International.[68] The founder, Craig Hill, realized he was spending a lot of his time as a pastor, walking couples individually through the same steps in healing communication problems in their marriages. He found he could be more effective in this if several couples could come together for a weekend workshop. They could focus more intensively and have a better teaching and healing experience. This approach led to the development of several healing workshops: Empowering Relationships, Overcoming Anger, Financial Management and Blessing Generations.

Craig Hill is a Messianic Jew who fell in love with the historic biblical Jewish family practices of blessing. He saw the emotional damage being done in non-Jewish families, where fathers and mothers do not intentionally pass on their blessing to their children. We incorporate either a fathers' or a mothers' prayer of blessing as the final prayer in many of our ministry sessions. Many of the people who come for healing ministry have been emotionally or religiously abused by parents, relatives or clergy. We try to follow John Sandford's advice to begin a counselling or healing ministry appointment with the same question: "Tell us about your relationship with your mother/father."

Our training workshop for Family Foundations International began with an interesting challenge. We were pared with complete strangers, told to pray silently, asking the Holy Spirit for wisdom about the other person. Then we were invited to share what we had learned. It was a new experience for me, so I was quite nervous. At the end of the listening exercise I shared some very vague and faint ideas that had floated through my mind. My partner was amazed. He was going through a spiritual crisis, and I had described it fairly accurately. He went on to share things with me that were right on. Like me, he was completely dependent on the Holy Spirit. I had learned a whole new approach to prayer ministry. Instead of having to rack my brains to think up clever questions to ask counselees, all I had to do was learn to really listen to the Holy Spirit.

We saw how this works out in practice later in a powerful healing ministry experience led by the workshop leader. The counselee was a rather frumpy and downcast looking woman in her late 30s. In the healing ministry we pray with our eyes open, so we can see changing facial expressions when we hit a spiritual nerve. The counsellor went into prayer with the woman. He asked the Holy Spirit to show them both a picture or vision of what was going on in her spirit. They both reported seeing a vision of a little girl sitting on her front sidewalk with a tricycle sideways on the ground. A very angry postman was towering over the girl.

The woman was reminded of a long forgotten childhood trauma when she had left her tricycle on the sidewalk. The postman had tripped over it and fallen down. As he got up and brushed off his uniform, he shook his finger at the little girl and shouted "You stupid little girl, you will never amount to anything." It was nothing less than a powerful curse that cut the little girl to the heart. This was a tall man (authority) in a uniform (more authority), putting a curse on her and defining her false identity. But she did not know it was a lie. Perhaps her mother or father were too busy to tell her that she was a beautiful, intelligent child of God. For the next thirty years, deep down in her subconscious or her soul, she was bound to act the curse and this false identity out. She had had trouble getting a good job, was unhappy at work and her marriage had failed. She had lived out the lie and never amounted to anything by worldly standards. Spoken words have tremendous power.

The ministry leader began by inviting Jesus into the picture. He asked the woman if she could see Jesus, and then invited her to ask Jesus what He thought of the little girl. As she wept softly, and the Kleenex came out for all of us, we knew she had an answer from Jesus. We could also guess what it was. We knew He would tell her that she was not a stupid little girl, but a beautiful, intelligent, perfect and beloved child of God, who would be very successful in life. Believing this lie, hard as it is to comprehend with human logic, was the root cause of her problem.

The Genesis story of creation tells us that "it was very good" (Genesis 1.31 NIV). God does not make junk. The girl, now an adult, had believed a lie from Satan, just like Eve. Even though she was only five or six, the rigid legalistic rules of the spiritual dimension empowered Satan to accuse her of a sin against God. The power of this lie was a curse over her. It could only be broken by taking her sin-guilt to Jesus on the Cross and asking Him to bear it for her. As the words of pardon were spoken over her, we could all see the burden of heaviness lifting off of her soul. Her facial expression changed dramatically. Her mouth went from a downcast expression to a smile of pure joy. Her eyes brightened. She looked radiant. It was quite dramatic. She had become a new person, with a new identity as a beautiful child loved by God. She had become a sign of the glory of God in the world — her real identity. Over the years we have found many people who were in spiritual bondage to the lies that they were no good, unwanted children or a failure.

For me the most powerful FFI workshop was "Empowering Relationships." This is highly recommended for everyone who wants to have a good marriage relationship. As a typical emotionally challenged man, I would also recommend it for all men who want to understand how women think and feel emotionally. For example, I learned that women have an emotional/spiritual second communication channel that is always on and runs parallel to their regular communication channel. It seems to work like radar, sending out a pulse every few minutes, always asking the same question: "Does he love me." Most men do not seem to have this second emotional/spiritual channel. They bang their fist in frustration and say "I told you I loved you last week!" The woman hears the message on her mental/audio channel, but she may be picking up a very different message on her emotional/spiritual channel. Women find this confusing, and tend to trust the emotional/spiritual channel more. When Lucille and I came home after the FFI workshop, our daughter Mary could see the glow on our faces and greeted us with the words "you guys are different!"

12.5 Spirit of Slavery

When I was on St. Vincent in 2014-15 as Visiting Priest from the Diocese of Calgary, we discovered another example of stolen identity. We were very busy Monday to Friday establishing a school library. It was identical in construction to the one I had established in Kenya in 1965, except now we had computers. On Saturdays we taught the Alpha Course to a team from all the churches on the Island. On Sunday I assisted or led worship in various churches. This gave us a lot of exposure to Caribbean culture.

One of the things we noted about the culture, other than the wonderful sense of community in the church, was that the vast majority of marriages had failed or were not very functional. In preparing for a clergy workshop on healing ministry, I had a word of knowledge from the Holy Spirit. Under the conditions of slavery in the 1800s, the men and women had been separated. Some of the men were taken to special camps to be used for breeding, but they were not allowed to develop a family relationship with the women. This must have been an emotionally traumatic experience. Both the men and the women must have been extremely frustrated and angry. They may have made vows and spoken curses which could have sown deep roots of anger, fear of commitment and mistrust. These men never learned how to be fathers or husbands because of the separation. The women had never learned to be wives and have a trusting relationship with men. The word I received from the Holy Spirit was "Spirit of Slavery." This spirit may have developed over the years into a spiritual bondage or even mental stronghold. This root would explain the modern fruit of men (and women) in the current generation, acting as if they were in spiritual bondage and unable to form committed loving relationships with their wives.

When I shared this revelation with the clergy during a workshop on healing ministry it was sadly not well received. Like most clergy, they had not had any formal training in healing ministry. This was traumatic news for them. The optics were terrible and I repent my insensitivity in not preparing them more softly. I was the only white person in the room. The (all black) clergy unfortunately took this as criticism rather than an important pastoral teaching. I learned that I still need to learn be more sensitive to other people. Other than this miscommunication, we had a wonderful experience in the Diocese of the Windward Islands and continue to keep in touch with our beloved Alpha Students. If you look closely at my photo you may see part of one of our beloved Alpha students in the background. We are all glowing in the photo as we had just come out of a glorious final healing Eucharist at the end of our Alpha Training Course.

12.6 Spiritual Depression

Depression is probably the most common and least understood form of spiritual wounding leading to a bondage. Psychologists and spiritual counsellors are still struggling to find a way to relieve people from the complete loss of emotional energy known as depression. Depression is a sign that the personal spirit has been exhausted and wounded to the point where it can barely sustain physical life.

My own experience of depression is limited. I can only share what I have learned from experience with others. One of my long-time friends went through years of psychological counselling, tried all the drugs and even had healing prayer without much success. Charles Kraft did actually help my friend through an exorcism as described below, but this did not deal with the root cause of the depression, broken relationships.

The good news is that the Rev. Tuk Su Koo, who had prayed with me in 1995 as described above, happened to be in Calgary visiting in 2017. He was able to spend several hours with Lucille and I and share his teaching on healing and delivering people from depression. He has developed an approach to healing spiritual depression that we have found successful. Rev. Koo explained that the root cause of spiritual depression is the unfinished emotional business hanging over a person from broken relationships. This unresolved emotional business leads to confusion, anger, bitterness, and un-forgiveness. Un-forgiveness, anger and jealousy are all serious sins that wound and pollute the personal spirit. These wounds act as doorways for oppressing demons of anger, bitterness, un-forgiveness and rejection.

Koo has developed a model which illustrates how spiritual depression is driven by a demon of rejection, which deceives people into seeing the world as split and unequal. This worldview leaves the person feeling rejected and swinging back and forth between two opposite perspectives of their place in the broken relationship. Rev. Koo calls these two opposing perspectives "Top Dog" and "Underdog."

When the depressed person sees themselves as the "top dog" in the relationship they are vulnerable to oppression by the spirits of domination, manipulation and control. These oppressive spirits confuse and weaken them, driving them further into depression.

When they swing to the other side in trying to understand the relationship, and see themselves as the "underdog" in the relationship, they are vulnerable to oppression by the spirits of fear, performance and indecision. These spirits also drive them deeper into depression.

Neither perspective can help them resolve and escape from the relationship and its prison of depression. This confusion is an exhausting experience as they swing back and forth between these two opposing perspectives of the relationship. They are oppressed by both sets of destructive spirits and become more and more emotionally exhausted. This in turn makes them more vulnerable to the spirit of self-rejection. Self-rejection then enslaves them to spirits of self-deprecation, depression and death. Figure 12.1 illustrates this process.

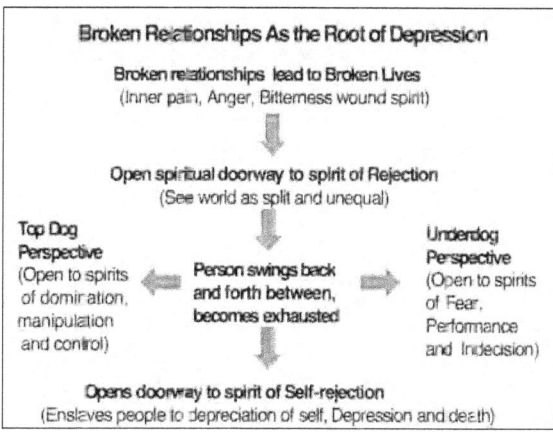

Figure 12.1

The healing process requires two steps. In the first our friend asked for guidance from the Holy Spirit and was able to identify two broken relationships that had never been completely resolved. She resolved these by bringing the healing power of Jesus to bear through the repentance, confession and absolution process. This breaks the spiritual power of guilt and shame that opens the door for evil spirits to oppress from the inside. The spiritual dimension operates on very legalistic principles. She needed to identify and address the brokenness of these past relationships in detail. This enabled her to identify the key or root that unlocked her from the prison of depression. Since the wound was caused partly by some un-forgiveness that this woman was unaware of, and unable to forgive from her heart, she had to ask Jesus to give her the will and strength to forgive. Jesus honours the intention of our heart even when we feel unable to completely forgive on our own. After she had done this, Rev. Koo was able to speak the words of absolution, and she verbally said that she accepted this forgiveness from Jesus.

The second part of the ministry was to plead the shed blood of Jesus over the each of the broken relationships, in order to seal and complete the healing process. We gave thanks to Jesus for His forgiveness and healing mercy, which had eliminated her sin-guilt, and protected her from further spiritual oppression. Over the next few months her life changed dramatically as she had been freed from spiritual oppression, and she had much more energy in her life.

Chapter 13

Exorcism: The Lost Gift of Christian Ministry

One of my most dramatic experiences as a person raised in a liberal Christian family has been the discovery of the reality of spiritual evil. Satan is mentioned often in the Bible but like many people, I did not understand or take evil spirits seriously. This is the key flaw in liberal theology. Liberals often both know and don't know (see "Self-Deception" 5 on page 67) that Satan is real. This works for Satan, but against the rest of us. Many people have believed the lie of Satan and demons as ancient myths and irrelevant superstitions. Many people seem confused. They are caught between extreme liberal denials of Satan and extreme evangelicals, who sometimes see Satan behind every tree, and do great spiritual damage by trying to cast out evil spirits without the guidance and authority of the Holy Spirit as described above. They miss the first part of Jesus mission statement. He was "anointed by the Holy Spirit" for His ministry. These misguided individuals have sadly discredited deliverance ministry, which was a central part of baptism preparation in the early Church.

My experience is that spiritual healing ministry is like scuba diving. It is fairly easy and safe on the surface. We help people through self-examination, repentance, confession and absolution to free them from the guilt and shame of sins. There is a natural progression in spiritual wounding. Un-forgiven sins cause spiritual wounds. These wounds are like doorways for the demonic. Demons gain a legal right to enter a person and deceive and oppress them from the inside. As in scuba diving, going deeper from healing ministry to deliverance ministry the pressure becomes more dangerous. More training, courage, experience and faith is required to free people from the oppression and bondage of evil spirits. Because of this, many clergy wisely avoid deliverance ministry out of fear of the unknown. Clergy are also nervous about being associated with the excesses and even fraudulent behaviour of some TV evangelists.

Spectacular movies, like those of Dan Brown and *The Exorcist* (a true but highly exaggerated exorcism story), have fed the popular liberal mocking of exorcisms as mythical.

Only recently has the Roman Catholic Church begun to take the training of priests in exorcism seriously again, and required every diocese to appoint an exorcist. In the Anglican Church of Canada, each diocese is supposed to have an exorcist and clergy are supposed to get permission from their bishop before doing exorcism. This is difficult as many of our more liberal bishops no longer really believe in oppression by evil spirits and demons. I find it quite sad that people like Dan Brown can attract a huge audience for movies about supernatural evil that are grossly heretical. Meanwhile, many churches that could be actually helping to deliver people from evil (as in the Lord's Prayer), are sinking into irrelevance and declining.

Our deepest learning on exorcism came at a workshop led by Dr. Charles Kraft at St. Peter's in Okotoks Alberta. Dr. Kraft began the two day workshop by explaining how he got involved in exorcism. He had gone to Africa as a Christian missionary. Almost immediately people started coming to him, asking for relief from evil spirits. He had not learned anything about evil spirits or exorcism at seminary. When he could not help these people and saw them going to the local witch doctor who could, he realized he had to give up. He had to go back to the U.S. and learn about exorcism, before he could be of use in the mission field. This led to an academic career at Fuller Seminary, publication of helpful books and a conference speaking and workshop ministry.

Kraft developed a gentler and more effective approach to exorcism than the spectacular violence in movies and in the experience of Scott Peck. We learned that evil spirits can be quietly and simply invited to leave by anyone, if their legal reason for oppressing the person is removed. I learned that things are very legalistic in the spiritual dimension. Most people would think for example, that a child or a born again Christian could not be oppressed or entered by an evil spirit. They would be wrong. Satan is a lawyer (you knew that), and without pity or mercy.

The idea of talking to an evil spirit is a little mind boggling at first, but biblical. A woman I know to be a very devout, life-long Christian apparently had a friend (code for "evil spirit"). I would not have believed you could talk to demons until Kraft's Workshop, where I heard her say in a very deep male voice, that was obviously not all her own: "I liked that!" This was in response to a question about her stillborn sister.

John Sandford disputes this practice as giving demons an audience which is complicating and counter-productive. He has instead learned to discern the root through the Holy Spirit, which is simpler and more reliable. I have tried both approaches and agree with John that exorcism is not really a big deal. Deliverance ministry and exorcism is often the only effective way of proclaiming freedom to the prisoners — as per Jesus mission statement (Luke 4.18). As the early Church expanded beyond Israel, almost everyone being baptized was coming from a pagan background. Exorcism of demons was a normal weekly part of baptism preparation. I am sharing the story of the Kraft workshop in detail as it may help others understand how exorcism actually works.

Dr. Kraft brings a team of prayer ministers with him who surround the exorcism with a holy environment of prayer and praise. Kraft begins with a long pastoral conversation. He tries to identify the name of the spirit (the root sin), and what may have happened in the person's life to give the spirit "rights" or legal permission to be there. When he knows the background, he calls the spirit to attention and takes authority over it in the name of Jesus Christ. He allows the demon to speak using the person's normal voice. Shouting, cursing and throwing the person around are specifically forbidden. The conversation with the demon may take another hour.

Kraft begins the dialogue by checking the name of the spirit (i.e., "Spirit of Un-forgiveness"), and asking what "rights" it has to be there. For example a spirit of un-forgiveness might say: "she has not forgiven her mother". If this is true, the conversation with the spirit is put on pause, and the person is invited to remove this "right" by repenting, confessing and accepting forgiveness from Jesus for that sin. Kraft then goes back to the paused conversation with the demon to see if there are any other rights (of demons to remain). It is meticulous, picky work, but it is effective. When all the rights of all the demons to be present are removed, they cannot resist and all have to obey the command, in the name of Jesus, to get into the little spiritual box, and go directly to Jesus for judgement. We saw three people's lives transformed over two days. Their faces changed to reflect the new inner spiritual peace, love and joy in their lives.

This experience taught me how legalistic things are in the spiritual dimension. For example there is no general forgiveness of all sins. This is bad news for Anglicans as we have a General Confession in our liturgy. Unless a specific sin is named and confessed (i.e., "anger at...," "hate of...," "envy about...," "pride," etc.) there may be no serious repentance and confession, and forgiveness may not really be possible. The take away is that each person needs to examine their life at home before the General Confession, to identify and repent specific sins. These can then be silently confessed as the general "things we have done and left undone" in the General Confession. This serious and specific confession in the heart by repentance would be more effective.

There was a final check during the workshop to ensure no other evil spirits are left behind. The spiritual doorways were sealed in prayer with the blood of Jesus. The deliverance or exorcism ended with a blessing prayer over the counselee. It is an incredible experience to watch.

My own experience in deliverance ministry gradually grew deeper as the need arose. Exorcism is a natural part of this ministry because we live, in the words of Craig Hill of FFI: "in a pagan culture on a demon infested planet surrounded by evil spirits." In the Lord's Prayer we ask to be delivered from evil. Many people confuse this with badness (natural evil). The Greek for the Lord's Prayer is very specific: "the evil one." It's a person and personal. Evil is live spelled backwards in case you didn't notice.

My most powerful experience of exorcism was with a woman whose ancestors were Hindu. She worked in a hospital with veterans who had been traumatized by combat many years earlier. She had picked up a demon that was oppressing her. Lucille and I listened to her story, organized prayer coverage for ourselves and celebrated a Eucharist with her. Then went through Dr. Kraft's steps as described above. We were really crying out to the Holy Spirit for help. First we first found out its name (Abadan the destroyer in Revelation). I did not realize who this was at the time. Abaddan (Death or the destroyer) is a powerful principality (Revelation 9.11). If it was not lying, we should have backed off as John Paul Jackson explains in *Needless Casualties of War*. it is extremely dangerous to take on a principality. We foolishly went ahead with the conversation, and by the grace of God identified its rights to oppress the woman. After we had gone through the Confession and Absolution process and removed all these rights, I took authority in the name of Jesus and ordered the demon to go directly to Jesus for assignment (and not touch anyone else or come back). We sealed the woman with the shed blood of Jesus for protection, and prayed for the infilling of the Holy Spirit. The woman was filled with joy and free!. It was the scariest moment in my twenty-five years of ordained ministry. Do not try this at home, without serious training and the support of a team of experienced prayer warriors covering you with prayers for protection and wisdom!

Chapter 14

Protecting Spiritual Life:
Taking the Long View

The final thing to know in discovering, developing and healing your spiritual life, is how to protect that spiritual life in a physically, psychologically and spiritually dangerous world. We all know how to protect our physical life by teaching children to beware of strangers, look both ways before crossing streets and obey traffic signs. But it is very rare to hear parents or even clergy, talking about protecting our personal spiritual life. Most people would probably think that going to church and being a good person is enough protection for spiritual life. This is prideful, dangerous and short-sighted. It is prideful because it is based on the false assumptions that humans are always intelligent enough to look after themselves and that our minds do not deceive us. It is dangerous because it ignores the supernatural worldview of the Bible and biblical teachings about the holiness of God, spiritual temptation and oppression and sin which can pollute and destroy our spiritual life. Finally it is short-sighted. It does not take the long view, as Her Majesty Queen Elizabeth would say.

To take the long view, it is helpful to think of our relatively short time on Earth as only a practice or training game, for our much longer and more joyful life in Jesus, in the spiritual dimension of heaven. The Apostle Paul teaches us that: "we also glory in our sufferings, because we know that suffering produces perseverance; perseverance, character; and character, hope" (Romans 5.3-4). This worldview assumes that all the obstacles we face: sickness, handicaps, fears, failures, temptations etc., are designed to help us develop spiritual relationship, character and strength. Just as athletes train for hours, pushing their muscles to do more, these obstacles in our lives push us to realize our limitations and our dependence on Jesus Christ and the Holy Spirit for forgiveness, hope, comfort and guidance.

It was my trying to understand why things go wrong, that led to my discovery of the reality of the supernatural dimension, and a deeper and richer personal spiritual life. The experiences of the past fifty years have taught me things you cannot learn from books. My rational mind could not really believe in, or comprehend, the healing miracles of Jesus, the gifts of the Holy Spirit, or the reality of oppression by evil spirits.

My experiences of the supernatural and love brought my slumbering spirit to life and opened of my spiritual eyes to see the role of Satan and deliverance from the mental strongholds of intellectualism and liberalism. I discovered the role of Satan and his demons in making things go wrong. The book of Job gives an interesting overview of the relationship between God and Satan, beyond the biblical warnings of temptation, sin and spiritual oppression. In the opening chapter of the Book of Job, God is showing Satan how devoted and successful Job is. Satan challenges God to take away Job's success: cattle, sheep, children and crops; and then see if Job still honours God. God gives Satan permission to inflict disasters on Job (but not kill him). This happens as tribal raiders kill his sons and steal his flocks. Job is reduced to sitting on an ash heap scraping his sores. For the next 28 Chapters, his friends torment him with pleas to repent whatever he has done or curse God and die.

Job knows he is blameless, refuses to dishonour God and cries out for justice. God is very impressed at Job's faith and restores everything — more children, more animals, etc. The part that is stunning is that Satan has to get permission from God before he can do anything. This may be a significant theological teaching. Many people either do not believe in the reality of Satan at all, or tend to (wrongly) equate him to God as an almost equal and opposing power. This passage helped me see Satan and spiritual oppression in a more positive role, as personal spiritual testers or trainers in a much larger training game. This training game may be an essential part of God's desire to create and develop holy people that He can have an eternal relationship with. This is consistent with Paul's teaching in Romans 5 that "suffering produces perseverance; perseverance, character; and character hope." This hope in Jesus Christ is critical to healing, holiness and a faith relationship with God.

The 1982 Star Trek movie *Star Trek II: The Wrath of Khan* included a very relevant teaching. Captain Kirk is being teased by his officers about his time at Star Fleet Academy. Apparently there was a final training exercise (the *Kobiyashi Maru* test) in which the cadets go into space in a starship simulator. They pick up a faint distress signal from the farthest corner of the Federation and go out to investigate (at several times the speed of light). The signal is from just outside the boundary in a no-go zone, but they decide to break the rules and help. As their starship arrives, they notice strange light patterns. Four enemy starships are de-cloaking and a battle rages. It gets worse and worse. Everything they try to do is not enough. They all die — except Kirk's crew. He apparently broke in the night before, and re-wired the computers so he could win. The real test of the exercise is not about skill, but about character: how well did you live and die? It's an important question for us all.

Going back to our body, soul and spirit model in Chapter 2 on page 9, we can now see that we are also tested by the demands and temptations of our ego and natural world, as well as the temptations and deceptions of Satan and evil spirits. Add to this our natural human weakness and self-deception, and it is not hard to see why things go wrong in our lives. This is why we are all dependant on the good news of forgiveness through belief in Jesus Christ, and on the gifts of the Holy Spirit to discover, develop and heal our spiritual life. I have shared my own discovery of spiritual life through Bible study, experiences of the Holy Spirit and healing ministry. This has been developed and nurtured through many churches, Alpha and Cursillo groupings, where I experienced Christian community, orthodoxy, relevance and outreach.

My final sharing is how Lucille and I learned to protect our spiritual lives from spiritual attacks. Like most people we had read many warnings about the need to cover ourselves in prayer before praying for other people. This is to ensure we do not pick up or pass on spiritual pollution through the laying on of hands. But we had not developed a daily practice of Bible reading and praying together. When we were in the Caribbean on St. Vincent in 2014-15 we were taught a dramatic lesson. We were living in a very nice rectory in Kingstown and had only been there a week. Everything was going wrong. Lucille could not get the washing machine or oven to work. We had a flat tire on our jeep and the tyre iron and jack had been stolen. Then our toilet became blocked and it took a week to dig up and replace the pipe to our septic tank. Nobody called or invited us out. Lucille was so discouraged she was talking about going home alone. Then we realized the nice young man who sat at our gate and waved to us coming and going, was probably a Rastafarian witch doctor and might be praying against us.

We put out an email SOS for prayer and got some helpful advice about witchcraft being common in the Caribbean, and promises of prayer coverage. We also started doing daily Bible reading and prayers together for protection. Within a week things changed dramatically. We got the toilet and tire fixed. We found a hose for the washing machine. A neighbour showed Lucille how to light the oven. Things went better on our both school library project and in advising the National Archives on standards. We soon got to know some people who became close friends that we still correspond with. We found a nurturing community in the Cathedral Prayer Group, Bible Study group and with our Alpha Course students.

While spiritual protection is critical for people trying to develop a spiritual life, the main challenge is overcoming the confusion of our "progressive" western culture. It is hard to *Go Spiritual* in a culture that is trying to escape from religious tradition and "go political." Way back in the 1980s, when I was a librarian at the Calgary Public Library, I had sponsored a ten part film series during Lent, based on the book *How Shall We Then Live* by Francis Schaeffer.[69] Schaeffer was an atheist doctoral student in Philosophy who undertook exposing the Bible as mythical as his thesis topic. In order to maintain his integrity in research, he decided to actually read the whole Bible to gather evidence. Like me, and many more people, he had a life transforming experience and became a famous teacher of Christianity. The book and film series illustrated how Christianity became corrupted through the centuries by politically ambitious church leaders and disputes over orthodox doctrine. This background helped me to understand how the truth of the biblical text, was manipulated either to avoid persecution by secular rulers, or to assert religious power and control over churches. Schaeffer used the term "true truth" to distinguish real truth from what different people might claim to be the truth. The point was that "true truth" is absolute truth. It is not debatable. It can be interpreted as an interpretation or opinion, but not as an alternative truth (as many people do now).

This practice of degrading the English language has continued down to our own time when everyone is confused by platitudes, politically correct speeches and spurious arguments. For example in one sermon we heard the argument that it was unloving to oppose "equal marriage" between same-sex couples. Really? Equal what? Equal to what? The consequence of these vague arguments is that people end up talking about completely different things to justify or support an argument that cannot be supported if you stick to the details of the real issue. In a Christian sermon the real issue is always "does this teaching agree with the received truth of the whole Bible about holiness, marriage and spiritual life?"

The consequence of this confusion of language and political discussion has produced a culture of uncertainty and confusion where many people are unhappy in their lives. Their lives may have no real meaning, purpose or joy. This is the main reason Lucille and I expand Paul's daily prayer for protection to include protection from lies, deception and spiritual attack. We do this every morning before we begin our day. The prayer is based on Ephesians 6.12-17. Paul's prayer advice is preceded by a serious warning that is worth quoting:

> "For our struggle is not against flesh and blood, but against the rulers, against the authorities, against the powers of this dark world and against the spiritual forces of evil in the heavenly realms." (v. 12)

Lucille and I begin our daily prayer time with a Bible reading, followed by thanksgivings for the blessings of the previous day and then we pray for protection, asking the Holy Spirit to come over us as:

1. The *Helmet of Salvation* to protect our minds (i.e., our souls) from deception (self-deception, human deception and the deception of evil spirits).
2. The *Breastplate of Righteousness* to protect our hearts (spirit) from deception.
3. The *Belt of Truth* (The Bible and revelations of Holy Spirit of truth) to hold us together so we do not fall apart in the post-truth culture we live in.
4. The *Shoes of the Gospel of Peace* so that we can stand on the Word of the Bible, and not be moved or deceived by false teachers.
5. The *Shed Blood of Jesus Christ* over us so that our sins will be paid for, and we will not be found guilty and vulnerable to spiritual attack
6. The *Shield of Faith* in front of us so that we can stand against the lies of the enemy of our souls.
7. The *Mantle of Praise* over us so that we can be (who God intended us to be), a sign of the glory of God in the world.

Our prayer time ends with prayer for all the members of our families, our church communities and those we know who are in special need.

This is how we can all gradually go spiritual through Bible study and personal experiences of discovering, developing, healing and protecting our spiritual life in Jesus Christ here on Earth. This experience just gets better and better. At some point our physical body dies, and we go completely spiritual in a new spiritual body, and live on more fully in the spiritual dimension with Jesus. My prayer is that this sharing of experiences and learning will help you overcome the confusion of our secular culture, go spiritual and find something more. Let me end with the dismissal and blessing that I use at the end of services and want to pass on to all my biological and spiritual children:

> "Let us go forth in peace to proclaim God's grace, love, forgiveness and healing to all God's children, in Jesus name."

John+, St. Luke's Day, 2017

Notes

[1] Francis Schaeffer, *How Should We Then Live?* (Old Tappan, N.J.: Fleming H. Revel, 1976).
[2] Ibid., 163.
[3] Watchman Nee, *The Spiritual Man* (New York: Christian Fellowship Publishers, 1968), 23.
[4] Ibid.
[5] "From Atheist to Preacher — A Life Changing Near Death Experience (Howard Storm NDE Testimony)," https://www.youtube.com/watch?v=Y9AjcfM75gI. Howard Storm describes his near death experience of both hell and heaven.
[6] John and Paula Sandford, *Healing the Wounded Spirit* (Tulsa: Victory House, 1985). 47 additional teachings may be found in *Transforming the Inner Man* (Mary Lake, Fla.: Charisma House, 2007).
[7] Ibid., 107.
[8] Ibid, 15.
[9] Anglican Church of Canada, *The Book of Common Prayer* (Toronto: Anglican Book Centre, 1962) 567.
[10] M. Scott Peck, *People of the Lie* (New York: Simon and Schuster, 1983) 150-202.
[11] Herbert Fingoretti, *Self-deception* (London: Rutledge & K. Paul, 1969), 69.
[12] Lucy Freeman, *Freud Rediscovered* (Westminister, Maryland: Arbor House, 1980), 22
[13] Ibid., 25.
[14] Ibid., 22.
[15] Ibid., 34.
[16] *Webster's Ninth New Collegiate Dictionary* (Markham Ontario: Thomas Allen & Sons Ltd., 1983).
[17] Fromm, 78.
[18] Bruno Bettelheim, *Freud and Man's Soul* (New York: Alfred Knopf, 1983), 70, 78.
[19] Daniel Goleman, *Vital Lies, Simple Truths: The Psychology of Self-Deception* (New York: Simon & Schuster, 1985), 8.
[20] Ibid.
[21] John L. Sandford and Mark Sandford, *Deliverance and Inner Healing* (Grand Rapids, Michigan: Chosen Books 2008), 282.
[22] Ibid., 280-308.
[23] Personal conversation with John Sandford on September 15, 2017 in Hayden, Idaho.
[24] *Good News Bible* (Glasgow: Collins, 1976).
[25] *Deliverance and Inner Healing*, 280.
[26] Ibid., 283.
[27] Ibid., 284.

Id., 287.

Id., 302.

Ibid.

[31] Ibid., 305-6.

[32] Ibid.

[33] Gresham Machin, *Christianity and Liberalism* (Grand Rapids, Michigan: Eerdmans, 2009) and free at http://reformedaudio.org/audio/machen/Machen%20-%20Christianity%20&%20Liberalism.pdf

[34] John Peterson, *Healing Touch* (Wilton, Connecticut: Moorehouse-Barlow 1981), 26.

[35] Sinclair Ferguson and David Wright, ed., *New Dictionary of Theology* (Leicester: Intervarsity Press, 1988), 317-8.

[36] Thomas Bandy, *Moving Off The Map: A Field Guide To Changing Congregations* (Nashville: Abigdon Press, 1998).

[37] Don Posterski and Irwin Barker, *Where's a Good Church?* (Winfield, B.C.: Wood Lake Books, 1965).

[38] Ibid., 32.

[39] Ibid., 37.

[40] Ibid., 21.

[41] Ibid., 40.

[42] Ibid.

[43] Ibid., 39.

[44] Ibid., 46.

[45] Ibid., 45.

[46] Ibid., 43.

[47] www.wholenessthroughchrist.com

[48] John and Paula Sandford, *Healing the Wounded Spirit* (South Plainfield, N.J.: Bridge Publishing, 1985), 105.

[49] Ibid., 107.

[50] Ibid.

[51] Nee, Watchman, *The Spiritual Man* (New York: Christian Fellowship Publishers, 1977), 167.

[52] Ibid., 89.

[53] Sandford, *Healing The Wounded Spirit*, 89-100.

[54] Sandford, *Transformation of The Inner Man* (Plainfield , NJ: Bridge Publishing 1982), 239 (revised and republished Lake Mary, Fla.: Charisma House, 2007).

[55] Nee, 153.

[56] Sandford, *Transformation of the Inner Man*, 237 (revised and republished Lake Mary, Fla.: Charisma House, 2007).

[57] Sandford, *Healing the Wounded Spirit*, 256.

[58] Ibid., 371.

[59] Kenneth McAll, *Healing the Family Tree* (London: Sheldon Press, 1982), 2

[60] *Transformation of the Inner Man*, 295-318.

[61] Ibid., 303.

[62] Ibid., 317.
[63] *Deliverance and Inner Healing*, 283.
[64] *Transformation of the Inner Man*, 310.
[65] Ibid., 314-315.
[66] Ibid., 315.
[67] Ibid., 310.
[68] www.familyfoundationsinternational.com
[69] Francis Schaeffer. *How Shall We Then Live?* (Old Tappan, N.J.: Fleming H. Revel, 1976) 163.

Colophon

The body typeface is Palatino Linotype. The typeface of the captions is Optima. Both typefaces were designed by Herman Zapf.

The material was typeset using the book package of the LaTeX 2_ε document preparation system and X\jTeX typesetting engine on an Apple iMac, running the MacOS 10.13 (High Sierra) operating system. It has been formatted for double-sided printing, using the A5 paper size.

www.ingramcontent.com/pod-product-compliance
Lightning Source LLC
Chambersburg PA
CBHW071826080526
44589CB00012B/930